I PRESUM.

Stanley's Triumph and Disaster

Henry M. Stanley 1874

I PRESUME

*Stanley's Triumph
and Disaster*

by
IAN ANSTRUTHER

ALAN SUTTON
1988

ALAN SUTTON PUBLISHING
BRUNSWICK ROAD · GLOUCESTER

First published 1956; reissued 1973
by Geoffrey Bles

This edition published 1988

British Library Cataloguing in Publication Data

Anstruther, Ian
I presume : H.M. Stanley's triumph and
disaster.
1. Stanley, H.M.   2. Explorers—Africa,
Sub-Saharan—Biography
I. Title
916.7'04   DT351.S9

ISBN 0-86299-472-1

Printed in Great Britain by
The Guernsey Press Company Limited
Guernsey, Channel Islands

THIS EDITION
FOR HONOR AND KATE

Preface

H. M. STANLEY'S greeting, "Dr. Livingstone, I presume?" is one of the best-known remarks of the last century and is a classic example of Victorian banality. Even during Stanley's lifetime it became such a *cliché* that people began to wonder if he had really said it, but to Stanley there was no more bitter truth than that he had done so.

Many things were more important in his life than his search for Livingstone, and most of his biographers, quite rightly, make no more than a passing mention of it. He was only thirty when he was sent out in 1871, and there were still several years ahead of him before he was to begin on the real work of his career—the exploration of the Congo and the founding of the Congo Free State.

But throughout his life nothing was ever so important to him as his meeting and friendship with Livingstone, and even at the time he recognized it as being the supreme experience of his life. When he returned to civilization and was laughed at for saying "Dr. Livingstone, I presume?" he was cut to the quick and would have denied saying it if he could, but it was already too late, for the expression had caught the popular imagination.

It plagued and haunted him for the rest of his life, and he was reminded of it even on the most solemn occasions. One of these was in 1890, nineteen years later, when he was at Oxford to receive an honorary degree. A large number of undergraduates had gathered to attend the ceremony, and as silence fell and Stanley knelt before the Vice-Chancellor, one of them suddenly called out, "Dr. Stanley, I presume?"* It was inevitable and obvious, and everyone laughed. But Stanley was humiliated, because he had no sense of humour and had never been

**Memoirs, by Lord Samuel, page 11.

vii

able to understand what the joke was about. It was a great personal tragedy to him that at the proudest moment of his life he himself had created it. For it developed afterwards rather like a game of Consequences. Stanley said, "Dr. Livingstone, I presume?", and the World said, "Ha ha!"

Acknowledgments

IT is not easy to write a book of this kind for the first time, and I suppose that no writer ever needs help again so much as he does when he is just beginning. Even the simplest date or quotation can be difficult to trace because of inexperience, and for this reason I should like especially to thank the staffs of the various libraries who have helped me. A skilled librarian will find in ten minutes a fact for which an untrained author may search for days, and I could hardly count the hours these experts must have saved me. In particular, Miss P. M. Downie, Chief Librarian at the Ministry of Education, has been one of these, and I am exceptionally grateful to her, and also to the staffs of all the following libraries: the London Library; the British Museum, both at Colindale and Great Russell Street; the Public Record Office; the Colonial Office; Rhodes House at Oxford; the National Library of Wales; the Flintshire Record Office; the Royal Geographical Society and the Wellcome Historical Medical Library. I thank gratefully, also, Sir Owen Morshead, Her Majesty's Librarian at Windsor, for finding the extract relating to Stanley in Queen Victoria's letter to the Princess Royal, and this is quoted on page 163 by Gracious Permission of Her Majesty the Queen.

There have, too, been many private people who have helped me with special problems, and without their detailed knowledge many important points would have been missed. Over questions concerning Stanley's date of birth and early background the Rector of Denbigh, the Rev. H. Davies, has been exceptionally kind, and so have the Rev. R. Thomas of Bodfari, the Rev. C. Williams of Tremeirchion and the Rev. F. Williams of the North Wales Evangelical Union, all of whom have patiently answered questions until they must have been exasperated. Equal generosity has been shown by Mr. John Pearson of the UMCA, the Rev. Father Th. de Vries of the Catholic Mission at Bagamoyo, Fathers White and Crook of the White Fathers at Ujiji and Tabora respectively, while

Mr. R. G. McCallum, lately Warden of the Livingstone Memorial at Blantyre, and the Memorial's founder, the Rev. Jas. I. Macnair, D.D., the distinguished authority on Dr. Livingstone, have both helped me repeatedly in every way that was in their power. I cannot forget to thank, too, Mrs. M. Varley of Oxford, niece of Mr. Tovey, who sent me the anecdote which brings this book to a close, nor to offer my thanks once more to Mr. George Burnham Braithwaite for sending me much valuable information and lending me books, nor fail to say to Major G. P. Daniels, grandson of Stanley's publisher, how much I have enjoyed our correspondence and how sad I am that this has come to an end. I am more than grateful, too, to my publisher for giving me the help and encouragement in the early stages of this book which every new writer needs so badly. Miss Pamela Taylor, my secretary, who has worked with me from the early chapters, has also helped and encouraged me in every way for many months, and I offer her my sincere thanks.

In spite of the help of all these persons, however, there are three people without whom this book could never have been written. They are Colonel J. W. C. Kirk, son of Dr. (later Sir John) Kirk, the British Consul in Zanzibar during Stanley's visits there; Miss Diana Livingstone Bruce, great granddaughter of Dr. Livingstone; and Major Denzil Stanley, adopted son of the great explorer. To them I owe more gratitude than I shall ever be able to repay. The private letters and diaries relating to Stanley in the possession of these three have combined to create as detailed and accurate a picture of his journey to Livingstone and of his reception in London on his return as it is likely there will ever be, especially since the Kirk Papers were unfavourable to him, and thus gave the necessary counterpoise to his own reactions and accounts. All these papers have been shown to me without any restriction or `condition, combined with much warm and generous hospitality on many occasions. My hope is that Colonel Kirk, Miss Bruce and Major Stanley will like this book, will forgive me if I have said anything with which they cannot agree, and will see the whole as I have tried to make it— a tribute to a difficult, lonely, and exceptional young man.

I. A.

Contents

PREFACE   vii

ACKNOWLEDGMENTS   ix

PART ONE: *The Triumph*   1

PART TWO: *The Disaster*   117

EPILOGUE   183

APPENDIX   192

NOTES   193

INDEX   203

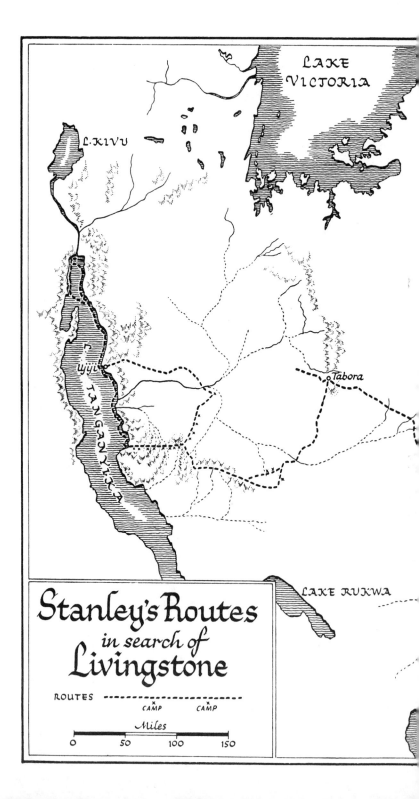

LAKE VICTORIA

L. KIVU

Ujiji

L. TANGANYIKA

Tabora

LAKE RUKWA

Stanley's Routes
in search of
Livingstone

ROUTES ------------------

CAMP   CAMP

Miles

0   50   100   150

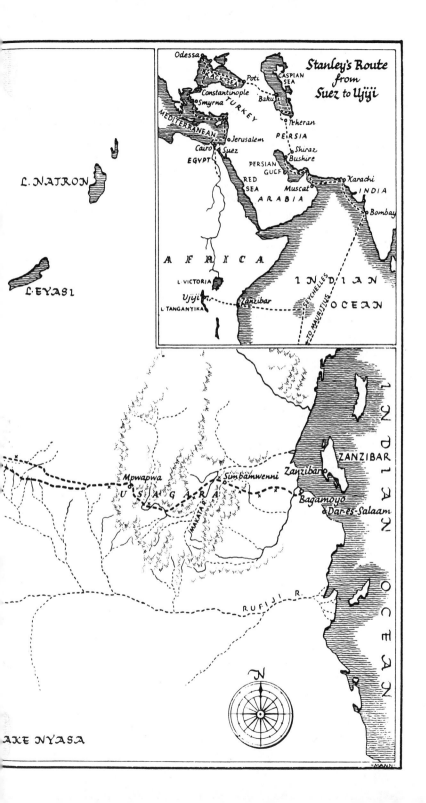

Illustrations

HENRY M. STANLEY, 1874 *frontispiece*

THE MEETING OF STANLEY AND LIVINGSTONE *facing page* xiv

UJIJI. THE MANGO TREE UNDER WHICH STANLEY MET
LIVINGSTONE IN 1871. (*By courtesy of the Royal Geographical
Society*) 82

REPRODUCTION OF EXTRACT FROM LETTER FROM
LIVINGSTONE TO SIR THOMAS MACLEAR AND MR.
MANN, DESCRIBING STANLEY'S ARRIVAL 98

REPRODUCTION OF EXTRACT FROM LETTER TO LIVING-
STONE FROM STANLEY 114

DR. LIVINGSTONE 130

HENRY M. STANLEY, 1872 146

JAMES GORDON BENNETT 162

THE MEETING OF STANLEY AND LIVINGSTONE

PART ONE

The Triumph

"But the great fact remains, and will be written on the page of history, that Stanley did a noble service to Livingstone, earning thereby the gratitude of England and of the civilized world."—Blaikie's *Life of Livingstone*, p. 432.

Chapter One

A T ten o'clock in the morning on the 27th of October, 1869,[1] Stanley was in his rooms on the second floor of a house, No. 31, in the Calle de la Cruz in Madrid when he received a telegram asking him to come to Paris on important business. He was one of the special correspondents of the *New York Herald*, and had been in Spain during the last seven months covering the civil war, which had broken out the year before and which had deposed Isabella II. He had just returned from watching a fierce outbreak of fighting at Valencia.

The telegram was from his chief, James Gordon Bennett, Jr., manager of the paper and son of the proprietor, and Stanley was delighted with it. Stanley was only twenty-eight, and bubbling with high spirits, and the faster he was whisked about the world by his newspaper the better he liked it. Without wasting a minute he dismantled his apartment, unhooked his pictures off the walls, packed and labelled his things, and hurried round to say good-bye to his friends, especially to two little English boys, Charlie and Willie. He left that afternoon on the Hendaye Express, and the moment he arrived in Paris the next day he went to see Bennett in his rooms at the Grand Hotel. Bennett had a corner suite on the first floor overlooking the Place de l'Opéra,[2] and Stanley went straight up and knocked on the door. It was about eleven o'clock in the evening, and Bennett told him to come in.

Stanley took a risk in going to the hotel at this time of night, as Bennett was strict about seeing people, and normally only allowed himself to be approached in his office at the proper time through his secretary. But Stanley did not believe in hanging about to see anybody, and he knew Bennett was just as likely to slap him on the back as fire him if he walked into his bedroom late at night without an appointment. He probably thought,

too, that he might as well get the meeting over, since correspondents were often kept standing outside the office for days
and then sent away without seeing Bennett at all, even though
they had been summoned from the other side of the world.

Bennett was in bed, but as soon as Stanley explained who he
was, he got up, threw on a dressing-gown, told Stanley to take
a chair, and gave him his new assignment immediately—to go
to Africa and find the famous missionary traveller, Dr. David
Livingstone, who had disappeared into the jungle three and a
half years before, had twice been reported murdered, and who
had last been heard of on Lake Tanganyika, about to explore a
cannibal country to the west. Stanley was to interview the old
explorer, find out what he had been doing and what his plans
were, make for the nearest telegraph office, and cable the story
to New York. He could have as much money as he wanted and
he should take a few extra supplies, in case Livingstone was
short of anything, but if the Doctor could not be found and was
convincingly reported dead, Stanley must make quite certain of
this and bring back absolute proof of it. As was popularly said
afterwards, he was to find Livingstone if alive, or his boots, if
dead.

Stanley's first reaction was to make sure that Bennett really
meant it, and that it would be an undertaking that the *Herald*,
rather than he personally, would be responsible for. It was said
that Bennett had no interest in the paper, and that as soon as he
inherited it from his father he intended to sell it. His father was
over seventy and, in fact, died three years later, just when Stanley was coming back from the jungle. It was an extremely wise
precaution on Stanley's part to try to foresee the consequences
and avoid being forgotten a thousand miles from anywhere.
Bennett never gave his special correspondents any kind of contract. You went where you were told and were paid for what
you wrote—handsomely, or sometimes not at all. All orders
were secret and, furthermore, Bennett merely used to make a
note of them in a private pocket-book, and never recorded

them in the office, or even mentioned them to his secretary. There was a well-known story of one of his specials who had been forgotten in Persia and who had escaped starvation only by pretending to be a dervish. The correspondent happened to be able to imitate religious ecstasy perfectly and, in the guise of a holy man, he had managed to persuade a passing caravan to transport him back to civilization. If this story was too good to be true, the moral was also too good to be forgotten.[3]

In Stanley's case, however, Bennett for once had gone about things in a normal way and had talked the project over with the *Herald's* London agent, Finlay Anderson, who is believed to have been the man who thought it up in the first place.[4] After that he had cabled John Russell Young, the managing editor in New York, to come to Paris by the next boat to discuss it.[5]

Bennett told Stanley this, and, so far as the sale of the paper was concerned, assured him that he had not the slightest intention of doing anything with it except to make it the best on earth, and that it could not be bought with all the money in New York—a statement which was more or less true, since his father had just turned down an offer for it of two and a quarter million dollars.[6] Stanley was satisfied, and went on to ask if he should go direct to Africa and start at once.

Bennett said Yes, but there were one or two things he could do on the way. He could go first to Suez to cover the official opening of the Canal, which was to be in a few weeks' time and was to be attended by the Empress Eugénie, the Emperor of Austria, the Crown Prince of Prussia, Prince Henry of the Netherlands, and distinguished representatives of every other country in Europe. He could then go up the Nile to contact Sir Samuel Baker, who was preparing an expedition to the Sudan, and in the process of this he could write a practical guide-book on Lower Egypt. After that he could report on recent excavations at Jerusalem, go to Constantinople, and from there run over the battle fields of the Crimea and make his way across the Black Sea, go through Georgia to the Caspian, and then turn south to Teheran. He could continue via Persepolis to the Persian Gulf, take ship to Karachi, follow on to Bombay, and finally make his way to Zanzibar and equip the expedition; when he got back from finding Livingstone he might have to go to China, but he would receive instructions about that when the time came.

The last thing Stanley did was to make quite sure that Bennett was fully alive to the probable cost: a previous expedition of the sort into Central Africa—that of the British explorers Burton and Speke twelve years before—had cost as much as three thousand pounds. What was he to do about that?

"Well, I will tell you what you will do," Bennett [7] said. "Draw a thousand pounds now; and when you have gone through that, draw another thousand, and when that is spent, draw another thousand, and when you have finished that, draw another thousand, and so on; but, FIND LIVINGSTONE. Good-night, and God be with you."

"Good-night, sir," Stanley answered. "What it is in the power of human nature to do I will do; and on such an errand as I go upon, God will be with me."

It was just starting to rain [8] as he came out of the hotel, and he went straight back to the apartment of a friend he was staying with—Edward King, a fellow American journalist—and told him he was being sent to Suez to report on the Canal. The following morning he went to London to see the *Herald* agent, Colonel Anderson, then returned to Paris, and he set off for Marseilles on 1st of November. Edward King came to the Gare de Lyon to see him off,[9] and Stanley laughed to himself as he thought of King returning to the safe boredom of Bowles' Reading-room [10] while he himself rolled out of the station towards the jungle.

Stanley's whole life was to be altered by the chain of events which had now begun, and once in Africa he was going to start the work to which he was to devote the rest of his career, to suffer stinging, lasting, and incomprehensible disillusion, and to undergo, in the meeting with Livingstone, the supreme experience of his life. And he was to do other things: to trace the Congo to the sea, to found and govern the Congo Free State, to precipitate the "scramble for Africa", to be the hero of England, and to become in the popular mind the prototype of all those remarkable men of the nineteenth century who explored the Dark Continent.

But at the moment of leaving Paris even the finding of Livingstone was more than two years in the future, and for the time being Stanley was supremely happy just leaning out of the carriage window and waving good-bye to King. The Marseilles express left at eleven [11] o'clock and, with glorious and increasing velocity, it picked up speed and carried him away.

Chapter Two

STANLEY was born on the 28th of January, 1841, in the town of Denbigh in Wales, and was baptized on the 19th of February in the parish church of St. Hilary's by the curate, John Jones.[12] In the baptismal register his father is recorded as John Rowland, farmer of Llys Llanrhaeadr, and his mother as Elizabeth Parry of the Castle, her maiden name being given, since she and Rowland were not married.[13] Stanley was christened John, after his father, and it was under the name of John Rowland that he spent the first eighteen years of his life.

The house in which he was born, a cottage now pulled down which stood in the precincts of Denbigh Castle, belonged to his mother's father, a butcher called Moses Parry, and his mother came there for her confinement from London, where she was in service. At about this time his father died, reputedly from the effects of a brawl in a public-house,[14] and as soon as his mother was strong enough she left Denbigh and returned to London. From all appearances she never thought of her baby again, for when she saw him for the first time ten years later, she merely stared at him and turned away, and when he went to visit her eleven years after that, she refused to have anything to do with him.

Until he was five he lived in Denbigh with his grandfather, quite happily, so far as he could remember; then the old man died [15] and he was boarded out with a neighbouring couple called Price for half a crown a week, paid by two uncles who had also lived with his grandfather in the same cottage. He stayed with the Prices for nine months, and went to the local free school [16] until his uncles refused to support him any longer and he was sent off to the parish workhouse of St. Asaph. He walked and was carried there by Dick Price, the son of his foster-parents, under the impression that he was going to visit his Aunt Mary, but when he was handed over to a strange man and saw the door close behind him, he was frightened and began to cry. He was put in a class with the two other smallest inmates and given the number 681, and it is recorded in the weekly indoor relief list [17] that he came in on Saturday, the last day of the ninth week of the quarter ending the 25th of March, 1847. He was then just six years old. It was many days, he said afterwards, before he learnt that in a workhouse the only result of tears was a beating.

.   .   .   .   .

It so happened that only a week after his arrival the school was visited by a representative of the Commissioners of Inquiry into the State of Education in Wales, so there is an exact picture of conditions as they were at that time.[18]

The workhouse itself was a large, bare building harbouring the poor of both sexes of the parish, and the school was held in two rooms on the ground floor and contained thirty boys and nineteen girls, whose ages ranged from about five to fifteen years. The schoolmaster was called James Francis, a terrifying man with only one hand who was consumed by fearful rages and who was later found to be insane and died in a madhouse. He was only thirty-two, and had been a miner until he lost his hand in an accident. He was quite unqualified as a teacher, even to the extent of being ignorant of English, although all books and lessons were supposed to be in that language, and although he was expected to punish the children if they spoke Welsh. The schoolmistress was his daughter, a child of only about twelve, who had been given no training in teaching at all.

The stupidity and brutality of this type of school are well known from books such as "Oliver Twist". In this case, among other things, the Board of Governors had refused to supply slates and maps, since they considered knowledge of arithmetic and geography unnecessary, and the lessons consisted only of interminable repetition of the Catechism and the Scriptures and "Dr. Mavor's Spelling Primer", the only secular book in the school, and one that had been out of date for fifty years.[19] Although the minimum daily period of study was laid down as three hours, the inspector observed that only two hours were allocated, and during much of this time many of the girls were nursing patients in the sick wards upstairs, while the boys were knitting stockings or plaiting straw. Such discipline as there was was that of the rod, and in spite of a clearly defined code of rules on the limitations of punishment—no child over fourteen years should be beaten, no child should be flogged until two hours after the offence had been committed and then, if possible, only in the presence of a member of the Board of Guardians, no child under twelve should be shut up in a dark room, and many others—Francis took no notice of these regulations and beat everyone who was within his arm's reach at the instant of provocation. But although the inspector thought that some children looked as though they had been harshly treated, he could not be sure that their pallid looks and drooping gait were not merely the result of having too little to do, and he reaffirmed the "inflexible rule" that all children should be employed ceaselessly from morning till night.

In many ways the worst of all the evils of the workhouse school was the perversion suffered by the children from having to live at close quarters with the adults, most of whom were the dregs of the parish of both sexes. Prostitutes used the workhouse for the cure of disease and as a lying-in hospital, the younger girls were put to nurse the babies, and the older ones nursed the women and learnt the tricks of the trade and became prostitutes themselves as soon as they left. The men took part in every possible vice, and the children slept together two in a bed, an older with a younger, so that from the very start the smallest were brought into contact with the bigger ones, who were beginning to understand and practise things they should not.

"It is impossible to overstate this evil [wrote the inspector]. It is a perpetual and active source of demoralization; it is irremediable, as long as the children remain in the work-houses. Even where they are kept in separate rooms they continually overhear the noisy and obscene conversation of the depraved portion of the adults during some portion of the day and in some instances they also sleep in the same rooms and inhabit the same day room. . . . As matters now stand the workhouses are, in most cases, nurseries of juvenile vice and idleness." [20]

Stanley's own impression was one of terror and bondage. He writes [21] fiercely of the shaven heads and fustian drab of the boys and the rough striped cotton dresses of the girls, the unchanging bread and potatoes and gruel, of the rigid routine of getting up at six and going to bed at eight, and of the furious ablutions on Saturdays in preparation for two interminable sermons the following day. Like everyone else, he was cuffed and flogged for the least stupidity or slowness, and one day, going into the mortuary, where there was a dead boy laid on a bier, and drawing back the sheet, he saw from weals on his body that he had been beaten to death, or at least had died after a terrible beating. To have been brought up in such conditions became an ineradicable humiliation to him, but nevertheless he realized afterwards that it had given him an unbreakable strength of character, and also, from the loneliness and the endless simple study and repetition of the Scriptures, an unquenchable belief and faith in God.

He was good at his books, and ended up by being head boy; the Bishop of St. Asaph gave him an autographed Bible as a prize for drawing, and a Miss Smalley gave him a drawing-book and some pencils. He was commended for his recitations and he led the choir of glee-singers, and ultimately, after the annual examination, he was pronounced by the inspector [22] to be the cleverest boy in the school. He was also a good mimic—

the first sign of a strong theatrical sense which influenced his behaviour throughout his life—and his impersonations of the Bishop and the inspector caused much delight to his companions.

But by nature he was touchy and silent, aloof and unfriendly, finding no one he could trust. He kept himself to himself, and probably did not do these impersonations very often. A Mr. Hughes of Llandudno, who knew him well at this time, when he was in his early teens, described him as having

"an indomitable will that really knew no impediment to its purpose—a full-faced stubborn, self-willed, round-headed, uncompromising, deep fellow. In conversation with you, his large black * eyes would roll away from you as if he was really in deep meditation about half a dozen things besides the subject of conversation. His temperament was unusually sensitive; he could stand no chaff, nor the least bit of humour. He was particularly strong in trunk, but not very smart or elegant about the legs, which were slightly disproportionately short." [23]

This chunky fatness made him an obvious target for the wits and bullies. The chairman of the Board of Governors, Captain Leigh Thomas, humiliated him one day by saying that he ought to be put under a roller, and a bystander at the blacksmith's once terrified him by remarking that he would be good to eat if he were stuffed with raisins. He could make no retort to these people, but although never very tall, with the boys he was an obstinate fighter, and was also exceptionally strong, and fewer and fewer dared to stand up to him. Finally he thrashed the last one who defied him, and from then on he held his place as head of the school, in class and out of it, until he left.

When he was ten years old, his mother, who by then had legally married a man named Robert Jones, came into the workhouse for a while, bringing with her a son, Robert, and a

* Actually his eyes were grey.

daughter called Emma.[24] It was then that Mrs. Jones and Stanley met, and she stared at him across the dining-room, "a tall woman with an oval face, and a great coil of dark hair behind her head".[25] He blushed when he was told who she was, somehow expecting to have known her instinctively and to have felt a sudden love moving in his heart. But she looked at him without interest and did not speak, and the disappointment and disillusion made a wound in his spirit which never healed. She stayed in the workhouse for a few weeks and then left, taking her son with her, but Emma was left behind. This little girl was there for several years, but although she rarely spoke to her half-brother, a long time afterwards, when he had achieved fame and glory, she is said to have tried to change her surname (as he had done) to Stanley, and perhaps during this period she was proud of him and loved him from a distance. Mrs. Jones, too, lived to think differently, and when she died in 1886 a brass plate was fixed to her coffin on which was engraved the proud fact that it was she who had borne "H. M. Stanley, the African explorer".[26]

He left the workhouse precipitately one summer when he was fifteen, not long after Francis had come back from his annual holiday to his native village of Mold, during which time Stanley had been left in charge of lessons. A new deal table had arrived for the schoolroom, and someone had marked it by standing on it, and Francis, knowing that he would get sharply reprimanded for this by the Governors, flew into a fury. When the culprit would not own up, Francis grasped a new birch and set about beating the whole school.

"Unbutton!" he roared at the first boy, dragging down his trousers and beating him. "How is this?" he shouted furiously as he came to Stanley. "Not ready yet? Strip, sir, this minute; I mean to stop this abominable barefaced lying." [27]

"I did not lie, sir. I know nothing of it."

"Silence, sir," he bellowed. "Down with your clothes."

"Never again!" roared Stanley, suddenly overcome by the

brutality and injustice, and quivering with a rage as furious and uncontrollable as the master's.

Francis grabbed him by the collar and threw him on the floor, but as the master bent over him, Stanley drove his boot into his face, smashing his glasses, and, snatching the birch, jumped up and beat him until he was senseless.

At last, stopping and realizing what he had done, he threw down the birch, and at someone's suggestion dragged Francis along the floor to his study, pushed him in, and shut the door. Then, with another boy, he walked out of the classroom, and on the pretence of going out to the wash-house, they both crossed the yard, slipped into the garden, climbed over the wall, and ran away.

In the St. Asaph Union discharge book [28] it is recorded that breakfast was Stanley's last meal before leaving, that he had been in the third class for diet, and that he had been a charge on the parish of Denbigh. Under the heading of "How discharged" is incorrectly written, "Gone to his uncle at the National School at Holywell",[29] and nothing is entered in the space under "Observations on general character and behaviour in the workhouse". The entry is certified by Captain Leigh Thomas, the man who had laughed at him and who suggested he would be better for being put under a garden roller, and the date is given as Tuesday the 13th of May, 1856.

Chapter Three

FOR most of the next two years Stanley lived with his Aunt Mary, an elder sister of his mother's, near Tremeirchion, the same Aunt Mary he had believed he was going to visit when he had been taken to the workhouse nine years before. She was a widow, and kept a farm, inn, and general store at Ffynnon Beuno, and he earned his keep by working as a shepherd and helping in the fields and at the bar of the inn. She was a joyless, severe woman, with a querulous voice and a "boney narrow face, dark with vexations",[30] and she showed Stanley no love, although she treated him with generosity and justice. If it had not been for her he would have been destitute, for after running away from St. Asaph he had tried to get help from his paternal grandfather at Denbigh, but the old man had only told him to get out, and the two uncles with whom he had lived as a baby had also refused to do more for him than give him a meal.

He was comparatively happy while he was on the farm, liking best the times on the hill with the sheep, when he was alone all day and could wander more or less where he wanted and enjoy the splendid view down the Vale of Clwyd to the sea. Aunt Mary's household consisted of her fourth son, David, who was fifteen—a year younger than Stanley—and the maid, Jane, and although these two liked him well enough, they always treated him as an outsider, and neither they, nor Aunt Mary, nor any of the neighbours who drank at the inn ever gave him a chance to forget that he was there on sufferance, the bastard son of a disgraced sister, and a penniless fugitive from the workhouse. Living now for the first time in a family, he realized what it meant to be loved and have a mother to rely on, and he longed for Aunt Mary to show him even the smallest sign of affection, but she gave him none.

In the spring of 1858 another of Stanley's aunts, Maria

Morris, who was married and lived in Liverpool, came to the farm on a visit. Stanley was now seventeen, and a plan to get him a job on the railway having just fallen through, he was about to be apprenticed to a cobbler, but Maria Morris took a fancy to him and told her sister that she thought her husband could get him a job in Liverpool with an insurance company. It was agreed that this should be confirmed in writing, and a letter from Stanley on the subject has survived, dated the 2nd of June, 1858,[31] addressed to Tom Morris, Maria's husband. In it Stanley says that he hopes he has not offended his uncle in any way, "as my Aunt thinks I have done", and trusts he may hear from him soon. Uncle Tom answered him satisfactorily not long afterwards, and at the beginning of August Aunt Mary bought Stanley a new Eton suit, and together they set off for Rhyl, where they caught a packet for Liverpool.

Stanley cried bitterly as they left, but he recovered his spirits as they came in sight of the Liverpool docks, which were filled with ships and bustling with noise and people. They went to an hotel, and in the evening Aunt Maria arrived and took him off in a cab, a long way through dim, gas-lit streets, to her home at 22 Roscommon Street. He never saw Aunt Mary again, and the last thing she did was to slip a sovereign into his hand and tell him to be a good boy and get rich quickly.

Uncle Tom was a merry, fat old gentleman who welcomed Stanley with enthusiasm. He had a carefree, jolly temperament and, although he had come down in the world and now earned only a pound a week checking bales of cotton at the docks, he had once had a good job on the railway, and still believed he had influence with various important people. But when it came to the test and he tried to get Stanley a position, he found he had been living on false hopes, and nothing came of it. Stanley had to look elsewhere, and he succeeded finally in getting himself engaged as an errand-boy in a draper's for five shillings a week, working from seven o'clock in the morning until nine o'clock at night. At first he was proud of himself and enjoyed it, and he and Uncle Tom used to have breakfast together at six o'clock, and laugh and joke while Aunt Maria and the rest of the household were still asleep, but the long hours were too much for him, and at the end of two months he collapsed and had to give it up.

Money began to run short, and Aunt Maria borrowed his sovereign, and took his Eton suit and overcoat to the pawnbroker's. She had two sons and a daughter with her at home, and again, as at Aunt Mary's, Stanley felt out of it and was constantly made to remember that he was a poor relation living on charity. After a further three weeks he got another job as errand-boy to a butcher near the docks, under the supervision of a ferocious Scotsman, and he spent his time carrying provisions to the ships. The towering masts, shining decks and romantic names fascinated him, and he talked to the cabin-boys and sailors, and envied their bluff manner and exciting life.

One day he was taking goods to an American packet, the "Windermere", and he went to the captain's cabin to deliver a note. The captain noticed how he looked about him with shining eyes, and asked him if he would like a trip to New Orleans as his cabin-boy, at £1 a month and a free uniform. This was a well-known trick, the boys finding themselves to be no more than extra deck-hands once they had set sail; they were treated so badly that they ran away as soon as they docked at the end of the voyage, thereby forfeiting their wages, which went into the captain's pocket. But Stanley had no idea of this, and accepted at once, hardly able to believe his luck. Aunt Maria and Uncle Tom did their best to persuade him not to leave, but they must have been thankful for such an opportunity, and Stanley had suffered enough dependence, and his mind was made up.

Three days later he set off for the docks for the last time. A steam tug pulled the ship into mid-channel, the sailors rowed alongside and climbed on board, and with ringing choruses they shook the sails loose, hoisted the topsails, and made them fast.

Lloyd's records show that the "Windermere" was ship rig, 1,107 tons, registered at the port of Boston, the master David Harding, and that she sailed from Liverpool five days before Christmas 1858.

The voyage across the Atlantic took six weeks, and the "Windermere" arrived on February the 5th, having run through a fierce storm in the Bay of Biscay. On the fourth morning out, after three days of prostrating seasickness, Stanley found himself knocked out of his bunk by the second mate and with furious insults told to get on deck and do some work. Stanley soon realized that there was no question of being a cabin-boy, the captain never spoke to him, and he settled down to the routine of scrubbing and polishing with the rest of the crew, acquiring the protection and friendship of the cook and of a boy of about his own age called Harry, who was an old hand and who had made the voyage before. He got his share of kicks and cuffs, but he was saved from the worst by the discovery of two young Irish stowaways of fourteen and fifteen who, from the day of their appearance, took the brunt of the mate's temper and swashbuckling curses.

The universal bad language and the fact that not even the simplest things were said without blasphemy were a complete shock to him. His life in the workhouse, on the farm, and in Liverpool had often been rough, but all the men he had known had controlled their tongues, and he had never met anyone who swore all day long as a matter of course. His whole education from the time before he could read had been founded on the Nonconformist code of narrow obedience to God's ordinances and literal belief in every word of the Bible. He prayed at night to the jealous God of the Old Testament who punished men's sins with hell-fire and damnation, and it never entered his head that anyone could ignore God and not suffer for it, let alone shout defiance at Him all day long and get away with it while living on such an easily destructible thing as a ship at sea. "I was about as good", he wrote of the time of boarding the "Windermere", "as religious observance of the Commandments can make one", [32] and he never forgot his shock at the profanity of the crew and at the fact that apparently God meted out no punishment for it whatever. "I belong to the Band of Hope and have signed the pledge",[33] he said to Harry when the latter took him to a bar in New Orleans on the first night of their arrival and tried to give him a drink. He gave in, however, over accepting a cigar, and was violently sick.

It was during this voyage that the effects of his illegitimacy, the stigma of the workhouse, and the fact that none of his relations had wanted him began to crystallize into a sense of inferiority which affected his behaviour for the rest of his life and made him so touchy and abrupt that people who were not prepared to be patient with him found him impossible to get on with. In his autobiography, which was written many years after his arrival in America, he said, speaking of this time:

"From this date began, I think, the noting of a strange coincidence, which has since been so common with me that I accept it as a rule. When I pray for a man, it happens that at that moment he is cursing me; when I praise, I am slandered; if I commend, I am reviled; if I feel affectionate or sympathetic towards one, it is my fate to be detested or scorned by him." [34]

It seems childish that he should have continued to think like this all his life, but on the "Windermere", whenever he asked especially for God's blessing on the ship or the crew, it seemed to him that the next day he was kicked harder than ever, and it inevitably linked itself in his mind with the times at the workhouse when he used to creep out of bed in the dead of night and pray for his playmates and then, if he was caught by one of them, was teased about it for a week.

At this time, too, he was completely naïve about women and had not the slightest idea, even in a schoolboy way, of the happiness or sensual pleasures which could be experienced with

them, or about the most elementary facts of their anatomy.
Shortly after he arrived in New Orleans he was sleeping in a
large bed in a rooming-house with another immigrant boy
from England. This boy turned out to be a girl, but they passed
several nights together before Stanley discovered it, and then
it was only after he had accidentally seen the naked breasts of
his companion and asked if they were not painful, as they
seemed larger than his own and inflamed by boils.

Harry, his friend on the "Windermere", having failed to
induce him to take a drink, lured him into a brothel—which
was an easy trick, since he had no idea of its function or existence. They were shown into a room, and Stanley was so upset when the girls appeared in their underclothes, and so horrified when one of them caressed him, that he ran out of the
house. The revulsion that he felt on that night came back to him
whenever he saw a prostitute afterwards, and his natural pru-
dery was so shocked that it was probably the reason for his
having no relationship with any woman until he married thirty
years later, while even his superficial dealings with the opposite
sex were always awkward and often absurd.

But if he was innocent about sex and prim about religion, in
other ways he had as much fun and high spirits in him as anyone else, and when he and Harry jumped off the ship on to the
quay at New Orleans for the first time, he flung his hat in the
air and danced away doing a couple of somersaults for the
sheer joy of once more standing on dry land and being safe.

On the fifth evening after arrival, having been made to scrub
and polish for five days with even more ferocity than usual, he
ran away from the ship without waiting for his wages, just as
the captain hoped he would, and he slept the night on the levee,
hidden between some bales of cotton. As soon as it was light the
next morning he got up, dusted his clothes, and made for the
main street and the area of the warehouses, hoping to find a job
quickly so that he might perhaps get a small advance of wages and
be able to buy himself some breakfast. He had not a farthing in

his pocket, but he had on a fairly clean suit, and as proof of good character he had the Bible which had been given him as a prize at the workhouse four years before, inscribed to John Rowland, the name by which he had been christened and which he was still using, and presented by the Right Rev. Thomas Vowler Short, D.D., Lord Bishop of St. Asaph, for diligent application to his studies and general good conduct.

As he went up Tchapitoulas Street the sun was already hot and the air was full of the smell of molasses and coffee. He walked quickly, looking eagerly about him, hoping to see a notice of "Boy Wanted", and watching the first few early negroes drowsily sweeping down their masters' stores.

Chapter Four

AT about seven o'clock Stanley came to a warehouse belonging to Messrs. Speake and McCreary, wholesale merchants, outside which was sitting a bearded, middle-aged man in a dark alpaca suit and a tall hat, reading a newspaper. He was the first man with a look of any importance that Stanley had seen, and after watching him for a while Stanley went up to him, and asked him if he wanted a boy. Something about the question or the way it was put seemed to catch the strange man's imagination, and he looked quizzically at the young Welshman and smiled and asked him who he was, whether he was a foreigner, and what the book was that was sticking out of his pocket. Stanley showed him his Bible, and the stranger read the inscription on the fly-leaf and demanded whether he could read and write. He gave Stanley his newspaper, and made him read aloud a political leader; he then pointed to a brush and a pot of paint in the store behind him and told him to mark some sacks of coffee with an "S" and "Memphis, Tenn." Stanley did twenty of these so quickly and clearly that the stranger was impressed, and said that perhaps he could do something to help him. He took the boy to a restaurant and bought him some waffles and coffee, then to a barber and paid for him to have his hair cut and his shoes cleaned, and then brought him back to the warehouse. He was only one of the store's agents, he explained, but Mr. Speake, the proprietor, would be along at nine.

When Mr. Speake arrived, the stranger spoke to him for a time in his office and then called to Stanley to come in. Mr. Speake looked at him and said he would give him a week's trial at five dollars—a sum so much larger than anything Stanley had ever earned before that he was speechless and turned, stammering, towards the stranger, not knowing how to thank him for his kindness.

"There, that will do. I know what is in your heart," said the stranger. "Shake hands. I am going up-river with my consignments, but I shall return shortly, and hope to hear the best accounts of you." [35]

The stranger left, and Stanley was put to shifting groceries on trolleys from the back of the warehouse to the street, ready for collection; and he worked hard, pushing the heavy loads as fast as he could, doing his best to keep back tears of gratitude. In the evening one of the slaves at the store took him along to a small boarding-house run by a young negress, who gave him a fine attic room with a four-poster. She made him feel at home and rather shy by coming upstairs with him at bedtime and helping him to undress, so that she could take his shirt and collar and wash them clean for the morning. Everything went well and at the end of the trial period of seven days Mr. Speake told him he was satisfied and engaged him as a junior clerk at twenty-five dollars a month.

This meeting with the agent was a piece of exceptional luck for Stanley, but six months later, when he had to look for work again, it was over four weeks before he managed to get anything at all. Overnight his engagement as a clerk changed him from a subservient slaving cabin-boy to a young man of independence with as much freedom and as many rights as anyone else. In England his accent and appearance had immediately given him away as a country bumpkin, and he had been treated accordingly, but in America he found he was accepted as an equal and judged only by his personal manner and his work. He soon felt the effects of this, and took on an air of pride and individuality, and held his head up, and was no longer afraid of being sneered at for being an illegitimate waif. When the agent came back a few weeks later and congratulated him on having done well and asked him to breakfast the following Sunday, Stanley thanked him warmly; a short while before he would have been so astonished at such an invitation that he would have been unable to think of an answer.

But in spite of his new manliness, he was still an odd little fellow, far less sophisticated than most boys of his age, innocent and gullible, thinking all men were what they appeared to be, and believing exactly what anyone told him. Although he had passed his eighteenth birthday, he was still dumpy in build and fat in the face, with a double chin, and he had rather a sullen, cod-like expression, with queer, short, thick eyebrows and penetrating grey eyes, strangely fierce for a young boy. He had a quick temper, and would flush with anger whenever anyone spoke sharply to him, brooding over it for days; but he never answered back. The strict discipline of the workhouse had taught him to speak only when he was spoken to, and he had grown up with such an awe of people older than himself that he was incapable of taking part in any conversation with them. The agent's wife, whom he met at breakfast the next Sunday, was the first woman of any education he had ever spoken to, and although she was probably only a simple merchant's wife, he was overwhelmed by her delicacy and refinement, and thought that if this was only a lady, angels, indeed, must be ineffable.

His relationship with this couple soon became one of close friendship, and he breakfasted with them regularly on Sundays, and went to church with them and for drives to the outskirts of the city. There were often other guests at these breakfasts, and for the first time he realized the immense gap that existed between his own class and that of more educated men, and hearing intelligent conversation, he was stirred to make efforts to equip his mind so that he could take part in it. He saved all his money and bought second-hand books, and he built a bookcase in his room out of old boxes, and read every evening halfway through the night. He learnt from the agent's wife about good manners and how to eat properly and speak politely and correct his Welsh accent and intonation; and he also learnt about baths and cleaning his teeth and his nails—none of which things he had ever before thought of doing.

When the agent's wife fell suddenly ill towards the end of the year 1859, at a time when her husband was away in St. Louis, Stanley moved into the house and stayed by her bedside, and when she died a few days later he was heartbroken.

Shortly afterwards the agent adopted him. Childless, and with a sick wife, he had often longed for a son, and Stanley's first remark to him outside the warehouse early in the morning, "Do you want a boy, sir?" had come back to him many times with strange poignancy. He had been a minister of the Church, and although he had given up religious duties and gone into business, he was still ordained, and one morning he brought Stanley into his sitting-room and read aloud the service of baptism, took water and blessed it, made the sign of the cross with it on the boy's forehead, and baptized him with his own names.

No foster-father giving his name to an adopted son can ever have received greater reward for it in glory and fame than did this generous, middle-aged salesman from New Orleans. Until this moment he had called his protégé John—John Rowland—as Stanley had been born and as he was known to everyone. But now the agent gave him his own names, Henry Morton Stanley—names that were to be made immortal by their new possessor and in their time carried to the ends of the civilized world to exemplify daring and courage.

The agent died within eighteen months, but Stanley used his name for the rest of his life, and until the facts became so well substantiated that he could no longer deny them, he threw dust in the eyes of anyone who tried to show that he came from Wales or had any connection with the family of Rowland.[36]

From now on Stanley travelled with the agent by buggy and steamboat all over the Mississippi area, learning the routes and channels of trade and the sources of supply, and making himself familiar with the whole of the agent's business. For a long time the agent had thought of setting up a store of his own, and now that he had someone to share it with and to whom he could

leave it when he died, he began to think seriously about it and
to consider places that might be suitable. Stanley showed himself a good pupil and quickly mastered the system of orders and
consignments and the detail of destinations and weights and
quantities, while on the long steamer journeys, when there was
no business to be done, the agent gave him lessons in the cabin.
Stanley was tirelessly instructed from morning till night, made
to get up at sunrise, and never allowed to be idle for one moment; but he loved and admired his foster-father too much to
resent this, and his intelligence was stimulated by it and he was
able to absorb all that he was taught. As had been the case in his
attic bedroom in the boarding-house at New Orleans, he was
driven by a fervent passion to acquire knowledge, and every
night he sat up reading until his father forced him to go to bed.
On New Year's Day, 1860, he was given a magnificent manuscript notebook, and he filled it with the daily remarks of the
agent which had made the most impression on him. He spent
most of the next nine months travelling about in this way, and
the spring and summer of that year were probably the happiest
of his life.

In September they were back in New Orleans, and there the
agent had news that his brother, who was a merchant in Havana,
was dangerously ill. For some time the agent had been thinking
of sending Stanley to a country store to gain experience in day-
to-day work behind the counter, and he had already made pre-
liminary arrangements for him to go to a friend who kept a
store at Cypress Bend on the Arkansas river. The agent now
decided to do this, since he felt bound to go to his brother at
once, and accordingly he fixed up for Stanley to travel to Cypress Bend under the care of a local plantation owner whom he
knew and who happened to be in New Orleans at that moment. There was the further advantage in this arrangement that
Stanley would gain first-hand experience of the territory, and
would be able to advise him whether there was any place in the
district in which it might be worth while opening up a store.

This plan being settled, the agent booked a passage to Cuba, and Stanley went down to the ship to see him off. Stanley's sorrow at this parting became another experience of such vividness that it never faded from his memory, and no boy leaving his family for the first time can have suffered more homesickness or missed the friendly presence of his father more than Stanley missed the agent who had given him the only period of security and happiness he had ever known. The agent's brother recovered, but the agent himself caught fever and died, and Stanley never saw him again; but at first he had letters from the agent regularly, and when these stopped, he put it down for a long time to the disturbance of the Civil War which had broken out in the meantime.

A few days after the agent had left, Stanley set off up the Mississippi with the plantation owner and joined the store at Cypress Bend. The period which now began was the last of the formative stages of his upbringing, and all his subsequent behaviour and manner and ways of dealing with men were influenced by it. It was a real hard backwoods life, with right and possession going to the strongest, and little gentleness or civilization except in the attitude to the women, which was one of exaggerated sentiment and chivalry. The community was the log cabin, the saloon, and the slave-worked plantation, and beyond the clearing in which these stood there was nothing but forests of huge pines and marshy wastes. Tempers were quick and the isolation bred an extreme sense of honour which had to be defended at the least provocation, and knifings and shootings were common. Every man carried a gun as a matter of course, including Stanley, who became an expert shot and could cut a piece of twine at twenty paces. The climate was very unhealthy, and he contracted a recurrent fever which he never shook off, and which prostrated him two or three times a month reducing him to a gaunt and yellow skeleton of less than seven stone. But the whole of life here was a fight against one thing or another—against Nature or one's fellow-man—and the general struggle toughened him into the decisive, implacable man that he finally became, able to look after himself in any circumstances, and never again content to let anyone stand unjustly in his way. To survive one needed energy and independence, and both these traits, already in Stanley's character, were developed and strengthened by this environment, coming at this particular time in his life. He was still something of a boy when he went out to Arkansas, but when he left he was a man.

He worked in the store at Cypress Bend for eight months, until early summer the following year, 1861, when he enlisted in the local company of volunteers. Abraham Lincoln had been inaugurated, the doctrine of freedom for slaves had been declared, most of the southern States had seceded, and the Civil War had begun. To Stanley the war meant primarily the enforced absence of his foster-father, who, if he were still in Cuba, would be prevented by the Northern blockade from getting back to New Orleans, and it was a long time before he found out that the agent had already died. Otherwise he was too ignorant of politics to become worked up over the issues, and apart from sorrow at the absence of his foster-father, his main feeling was regret at the dislocation of life and the stupidity of finding that all his friends in the North had suddenly become enemies. He did not enlist straight away, and did so only after being sent a negress' petticoat—the equivalent of a white feather. He records this incident in his autobiography to make the point that he still felt enough of a foreigner not to regard himself as personally involved in the fight, and that in the end he allowed himself to be pushed into it. This is an important point, because at a later date, after being taken prisoner, he enlisted on the other side—a change of loyalties which would be hard to explain in the ordinary way. But in cold blood he did not feel himself particularly bound to one party or the other.

Having joined up, however, he became as fierce a patriot as anyone else, and when his company marched down to the boat and steamed off up the Arkansas river towards the main point of mobilization at Little Rock, he was intoxicated by the fare-wells of the crowd and the romance and heroism of marching to war and death for one's country. At the end of July his company, the Dixie Greys, was sworn in for twelve months to the 6th Arkansas Regiment of Volunteers under command of Colonel Lyons, and, like any boy who has just joined up, he marched enthusiastically about with his rifle over his shoulder, and joined his messmates in the evenings in hilarious and melancholy songs.

Ten months later on the 7th of April, 1862, the second day of the Battle of Shiloh, he was taken prisoner, having been struck by a bullet the day before, but luckily on the clasp of his belt, so that he was only winded. It was his first experience of being under fire, there were heavy casualties on both sides, and the sudden death of so many comrades made him feel that all he had learnt of the mercy and goodness of God was nothing but nonsense. It was not until ten years later, in the prolonged soli-tude of the African jungle, that he recovered some of his earlier strong belief. He was taken to a prisoner-of-war camp near Chicago, where every day in appalling conditions he saw men die in dozens of dysentery and typhus, until at last, to escape death, he allowed himself to be persuaded to join the Federals. He did this in June, but although he got out of the camp alive, he could scarcely walk, and was worse than useless to his new commanders. After two weeks in hospital he was invalided out and turned loose into the countryside near Harper's Ferry. He managed to reach a farm-house, and then collapsed, and al-though he was given every care and kindness, he was not fit enough to leave for more than two months.

He had lost everything he owned, including his most valued possession, a daguerreotype of his foster-father with a lock of his grey hair which he used to take out of his pack and look at on Sundays; he had not heard from him for more than a year, and it was impossible to get to New Orleans to search for him. He decided to go back to Wales and visit his mother, and after working at the harvest in Maryland and then on an oyster schooner, he signed on with a ship, the "E. Sherman", and reached Liverpool in November and made for Denbigh. But he was gaunt and dirty, and his mother received him sourly, put him up for the night, gave him a shilling, and told him to go back where he came from. He returned to New York, joined the Merchant Navy, and sailed for Cuba in the hope of finding his foster-father. But he learnt there that the agent had died of fever a few weeks after he had arrived, almost two years before.

Chapter Five

FOR the next seven years Stanley drifted about the world, never in one place for more than a few weeks, travelling from beyond the Rocky Mountains to the Mediterranean, involved in battles and storms at sea, wars with Red Indians and fights with Turkish bandits.

After he left Cuba he worked on various merchant ships running between the eastern seaboard of America and Italy, until he was shipwrecked off Barcelona in May 1863, and swam ashore, the only survivor. Following this, his movements for the next ten months are unrecorded, except that he made his way back to New York and lodged with a judge in Brooklyn. The judge got drunk one evening and attacked his wife with a hatchet, and Stanley spent the whole night holding him off. But the wife gave Stanley no thanks and instead abused him because he forgot himself in the excitement and lit a cigar in the parlour.

In July 1864 he enlisted once more in the Federal forces, this time in the Navy,[37] on the U.S.S. "Minnesota", and in December was present at the first attack on Fort Fisher, an attack which failed, but during which he swam five hundred yards under fierce fire, tied a rope to an abandoned Confederate ship, and secured her as a prize. A few weeks later he took part in the second assault on the fortress, and afterwards wrote his impressions of both these engagements and sent them to a newspaper.

He was well paid for these articles, and their publication opened his eyes to a profession for which he had a natural talent, and in February 1865 he absconded from the Navy and went to work in New York as a journalist, probably for the *New York Evening Post*. From there he went west as a free-lance reporter, travelling all over the frontier country beyond the Rockies, and finally coming east again a year later, in May 1866, floating seven hundred miles from Denver to Omaha City down the River Platte on a home-made raft with a friend called Cook. By the time he reached New York, he and Cook had decided on an expedition to Turkey and, persuading a former shipmate—a young boy of nineteen called Lewis Noe—to join them as a manservant, they sailed from Boston on the 11th of July.

They reached Smyrna without incident at the beginning of September, and having bought horses and other necessities, set off towards the interior. After lunch on the first day, when Stanley had left camp for a stroll, Lewis Noe saw that Cook had fallen asleep under a bush, and had the idea of setting fire to it to give him a fright. This joke came off, but the fire got out of control and destroyed a large area of vineyards. Stanley and Cook were seized by the inhabitants, and Stanley only managed to placate them with great difficulty. Noe escaped, but when Stanley found him the next day he gave him a sound thrashing. Six days later they were ambushed by bandits, robbed, stripped, beaten, and Noe, who was very girlish and small, was brutally treated. They were bound and left in a cave for the night and the next morning they were dragged into a wood to be executed. But at the last moment, with the promise of a large ransom, Stanley managed to persuade the bandits to take them to the nearest magistrate, and, once there, he turned the tables on his captors and got them thrown into prison.

But Stanley failed to recover any of the money or equipment which had been stolen from Cook and himself, and was forced to abandon the expedition and go to the American Minister at Constantinople for help. This diplomat, Mr. Joy Morris, immediately protested about the incident to the Turkish Government and lent the party £150, a kindness for which he was ill rewarded, since Stanley gave him in exchange a bank draft that was worthless. But the Minister recovered his money from the £360 reparations which were ultimately awarded to the expedition, and he lived to become an admirer of Stanley's, and bore him no ill will. The three travellers stayed at Constantinople for two months to attend the trial of the bandits, who were convicted and punished, and in November Stanley and Noe left for Marseilles and journeyed to Liverpool via Paris, while Cook returned to America.

In Liverpool Stanley stayed with Uncle Tom, and he went again to Denbigh to see his mother, who, as he was better dressed this time and wanted nothing, appears at least to have suffered his visit, while possibly she even accepted it with pride. His previous reception had taught him a lesson and shown him that it was no good expecting anything from her unless he stood up for himself, so he put on uniform and gave out that he was still in the American Navy, that his ship had been visiting Constantinople, and that he was in England on furlough. To substantiate this he signed his name in the visitor's book at Denbigh Castle, "John Rowlands, formerly of this Castle, now Ensign in the United States Navy", and went to Shrewsbury and had his photograph taken in uniform. He left Liverpool again in January 1867, and once more sailed for New York, but before he did so he had the fun of visiting his old school in the workhouse at St. Asaph, where he stood the boys a free tea of buns and cakes, and gave them an uplifting lecture on the virtues of diligence and the rewards of hard work.[38]

Stanley was sufficiently well known in American newspaper circles by this time to be able to get a good job. When he reached New York he was engaged by the *Missouri Democrat*, and in April sent as a special correspondent with General Hancock. This General had been despatched by Congress to Colorado with a strong force to subdue the Sioux Indians, who were resisting more and more fiercely as the endless flow of emigrants pushed them farther and farther off their hunting grounds. Stanley met Mark Twain and Joseph Pullitzer on this assignment, both of whom were working as journalists in St. Louis, and when Hancock's expedition was followed by a peace commission under General Sherman, Stanley was accredited to him. This period of fighting and meeting the Indians lasted for eight months and was one of danger and excitement—just the kind of life Stanley liked—and he thoroughly enjoyed himself, and from watching General Sherman deal with the chiefs he gained first-hand experience in negotiating with primitive people which was of great value to him later on in Africa. His assignment came to an end in December 1867, and he made his way back to New York to look for another job.

After applying for work to one or two editors without success, he went to the offices of the *New York Herald* and managed to get an interview with James Gordon Bennett, Jr. This was a good start, since Bennett was unapproachable in the ordinary way, even to his staff. Although the two men were vastly different in background, since Bennett's father was a millionaire, they were exactly the same age and had much in common— drive, ability, and imagination—and Bennett saw at once that Stanley was the type of man he could use. He told him he had no vacancies at that moment, but congratulated him on the reports he had sent back about Hancock and Sherman, and thought he might be able to offer him something later.

In Abyssinia the British Government were about to undertake a punitive expedition against King Theodore, who had been maltreating British subjects and had thrown the Consul into gaol. Stanley suggested that since the *Herald* could not engage him on a salary, perhaps Bennett would give him credentials as a personal representative, and he would go to Abyssinia and report the campaign at his own expense. He would offer anything he wrote to the *Herald* first, and would sell it elsewhere if it was refused. Bennett agreed to this with the reservation that Stanley wrote exclusively for the *Herald*, and added that if he did well he would be given a permanent post at the end of the campaign. He gave him a letter to the *Herald* agent in London, and Stanley sailed from New York two days later.

To work for the *New York Herald* was the aim of almost every journalist in America, and Stanley was in high spirits, and felt that at last he had left the poverty of the workhouse and was beginning on the road to the achievement of his ambition. He spent New Year's Day, 1868, in Paris, where he wrote a note of greeting to his former friend in Turkey, Lewis Noe, "prince of boys and best of companions. In your rejoicings forget not the exiled friend and brother. Henry." A month later he reached Annesley Bay on the Red Sea, where the British expeditionary force was assembling.

This famous campaign, conducted by General Sir Robert Napier, came to a spectacular close three months later, in April, with the fall of Magdala and the suicide of the Emperor Theodore; and as the victorious troops swarmed into the enemy stronghold, Stanley was seen by a fellow journalist capering up and down waving a bloody rag, which he shouted out was part of the Emperor's shirt. A few moments later the journalist saw the body of the Emperor lying on the ground, but unfortunately for Stanley all the Emperor's clothes were still intact.[39] General Napier refused to allow Stanley to send back a special messenger with the news of the victory, and forced him to use the same facilities as everyone else, which in this case were the bags of the Government courier. But Stanley was determined to do better than that and, unlike the rest of his colleagues, who were now taking things easy, he followed the courier to the coast and left for Egypt by the same steamer. At Suez, by reason of a private arrangement which he had made with the telegraph office on his way up three months earlier, he succeeded in getting his despatches sent first. As soon as the last word of these despatches had been sent the cable broke somewhere on the sea-bed, beyond Alexandria and, as a result, General Napier's official communiqués and the reports of all the other correspondents had to go by ship as far as Malta. By this piece of foresight and luck Stanley achieved a first-rate scoop, and the *New York Herald* had news of the end of the war nearly three weeks before the British Government or any other newspaper. Bennett was delighted, and kept his word, immediately engaging Stanley as a permanent member of the staff.

This success went to Stanley's head, and he decided to get married. A few weeks afterwards he met a girl called Virginia on the Island of Syra near Crete. She seemed delectable, and when her father and mother objected to him as a suitor, he applied for help to a former official of the Egyptian Government, Hekekyan Bey.

"Dear Sir," he wrote on the 14th of September, 1868. "I want you to do me a favor. I am in love. The object is a Greek girl, steeped in poverty, but famous for her beauty. She is cursed with rather obnoxious parents, but I risk all and wish to marry her.

". . . Upon receipt of this will you be kind enough to write at once and state to them that by refusing me they have lost a most eligible offer and if any unhappiness is the result they have no one to blame but themselves." [40]

But Virginia's parents refused to understand what was good for them, and, in spite of the Bey's support, Stanley was rejected.

Shortly afterwards he went to London and met a plump Welsh girl, the daughter of a Denbigh solicitor who was staying in the same hotel. He determined to try again with her, but for the second time the parents snubbed him, and all he managed to do was to send her one gigantic love letter.[41]

Only a few months now lay ahead before Stanley was to receive the telegram in Madrid which was to summon him to Paris. In these months he moved about between London, Spain, and the Middle East, always in circumstances of danger and excitement, and never in one place for more than a few weeks—the life he liked and was used to, free and restless, with its success depending mostly on himself. "It is only by railway celerity that I can live," [42] he wrote in a letter to a friend during this time—an expression that was typical of his writing at its worst, which was always fatuous when it was meant to be telling, and full of facetious banalities. But there was truth in the analogy all the same, for he loved the speed and movement which the railway symbolized for his age, and he was fascinated by the spectacle of the vast new steam engines flying implacably towards their chosen destinations. In a way, they did reflect his character with their iron force, crushing and thrusting aside anything that got in their path.

Only two other things happened to him during this final period which had any influence on his character and future circumstances, the more important of which was his association with the officers of General Napier's army and the other newspaper correspondents who were following the campaign. Only a few years before, in the Crimea, William Howard Russell of *The Times*, the first man ever to be sent by a newspaper to report on a campaign, had been treated with astonishing rudeness by the military command and had written that no more notice had been taken of him than if he had been a crossing-sweeper. But he had also written with force and bitterness of the frightful muddle of the medical organization and of the terrible suffering caused to the men by it, and he had enraged military opinion, which was still in no mood to welcome the representatives of newspapers, whom they considered as no more than civilian snoopers. But over and above this, the officers of General Napier's army were the first educated and upper-class Englishmen Stanley had ever met, and he was taken completely by surprise by the coldness and formality of their manners. The English habit of reserve bewildered and mortified him and although, when he understood it, he admired it enormously and disciplined his temper ruthlessly to achieve it himself, on first acquaintance it increased his natural touchiness so much that, dating from this time, he looked upon every Englishman as a potential snob who would squash him if he had the opportunity, and whose every remark was likely to contain a sneer. Although General Napier himself treated him with friendliness and courtesy, a typical reaction of the younger officers was that of a cornet in the Scinde Horse to whom Stanley passed a remark and who drew back several feet and retorted, "Whom have I the honour to address?" Another young officer whom Stanley met one morning on horseback in the remote wilds and to whom he called "Good morning" only screwed in an eyeglass, looked at him, and rode away without saying anything. As an American, and a rugged one at that, Stanley appeared the sort of person one only read about in *Blackwood's Magazine*, who lived in a log cabin on the prairie and shot Red Indians, and to the provincial young subalterns he was not so much a man as an exhibit from a circus.

Stanley's reception by the Press contingent, among whom were Lord Adare and G. A. Henty, was different, although the result was the same. In Europe, except in financial circles, the *New York Herald* was considered the most scandalous and vulgar purveyor of gossip and trash in existence. That it should send a correspondent to follow a serious campaign by the British army in a country that probably none of its readers had ever heard of was a farce and almost an impertinence, while Stanley's unfashionable dress and discordant American accent gave his colleagues plenty of reason for laughter. Theirs was more good-natured than the amusement of the officers, and it stopped altogether when they realized Stanley's experience and ability, but while it lasted it hurt him just the same.

It is certain that he would have been saved many mistakes of gaucherie and conduct in later years, including a feverish nervousness at the moment of meeting Livingstone, which had fatal consequences for him, if he had been able to laugh off this initial coldness with which every foreigner who is introduced to a certain type of Englishman is liable to be received. In the final adjustment of his character this was one of the most important and unfortunate encounters in his life.

But if he was wounded in his dealings with people in one direction during this time, he had luck in another way in making contact with the American Consul in Zanzibar, Francis R. Webb, a former United States naval captain, without whose

assistance two years later he would have been helpless. Towards
the end of 1868 a rumour started in Bombay and found its way
to London that Dr. Livingstone would shortly return to civilization, coming out of Africa either at Zanzibar or down the
Nile. Stanley was sent to check this—an assignment not to be
confused with the one a year later which started with Bennett
in Paris, but just a routine job: to follow up the rumour and report. Stanley went first to Suez, where he could find out nothing but ran into a man called Macgregor, who subsequently became famous for his expeditions in a canoe called the "Rob
Roy". Macgregor cornered him and bored him with talk about
his canoe, but Stanley suffered it and was rewarded by a letter
of introduction to Livingstone, a letter which he never needed
to use but which might easily have been useful. He then went
up to Aden, and from there wrote to the American Consul at
Zanzibar explaining that he was on the *Herald* and that he was
trying to get news of Livingstone. Webb answered him on the
26th of December, 1868, assuring him that, so far as anyone
knew, there was no truth in the rumour and that there was no
likelihood of Livingstone appearing at Zanzibar or anywhere
else. This turned out to be correct, and in February Stanley was
recalled from Aden and sent to Spain to the civil war. He was
disappointed at the failure of this mission, but he had fixed himself in the mind of Webb as being a man on the *Herald* interested in Livingstone, and from the point of view of the circumstances lining themselves up, this was the final move that
was necessary before all the arrangements should be completed.

In appearance at this time Stanley was an odd little man with
black hair and a red face, not attractive at first sight, although
there was something about him that stuck in people's minds,
and he was obviously a man of determination. He was clean-
shaven, except for a dark, wispy moustache, and his face was
boyish, strangely florid, and almost completely round, with a
double chin, a well-proportioned nose, and a long, full mouth
with drooping ends. His eyes were light grey and curiously

penetrating, set straight and wide over high cheekbones; his eyebrows were dark and oddly short and his hair was dark also, long and thick and slightly wavy, and parted on the left. He was only five feet five inches in height, but was heavily built, tremendously deep and wide in the chest and shoulders and weighed 165 lb.—or only just under twelve stone.[43] His feet were rather large, but his hands were small and red, and he wore a signet ring on the little finger of the left hand.

He was always badly dressed, rather uncouth in his general behaviour, exceedingly shy, entirely lacking in small talk, but he had a strong comic sense and could be amusing and congenial when with his friends, although he was quick-tempered and completely without a sense of humour about himself. He spoke with a pronounced American accent which lapsed into the higher sing-song intonation of his childhood Welsh when he became excited. He smoked a pipe and cigars, and took a drink when one was offered to him, but he was drunk only once in his life—when he was twenty-five—and he was so disgusted with himself afterwards that he never drank alcohol for choice again and was rather a prig about anyone who did. He was also a prude about women, being completely inexperienced with them and finding the idea of sexual intercourse repulsive. He was also rather tight-lipped over the weaknesses of others, being himself gifted with ferociously determined will-power. Physically, too, he was unusually strong, and had almost superhuman powers of endurance and reserves of energy, so that he could go without food or sleep for days, and even in the tropics work or march for a length of time and with a persistence that would normally be possible only for the toughest native. He had also an exceptional memory, and among his more normal accomplishments were the ability to draw well and an aptitude for languages, while he was in addition a good horseman, a strong swimmer, and an accurate shot.

All these characteristics combined to give him in public an air of dogged self-assurance, and in private a certain boyish exuberance. If, at the age of twenty-eight—just before he set off in search of Livingstone—he seemed odd and common to upper-class Englishmen, to his American contemporaries, such as Joy Morris, the American Minister at Constantinople, whom he met again just before he started, he appeared as a "perfect man of the world".[44] Edward King—the journalist with whom he stayed in Paris—admired him too. King became a friend for life, and described him as "honest, original and wise".[45]

And with Stanley's appointment to Spain, all the events that were to happen to him to equip him for the search for Livingstone—all the chances, training, and experience, all the circumstances except the final one of being summoned to Paris and receiving his orders—had occurred. He was in the front rank as a journalist, of proved reliability and determination, a fast and lucid writer, with the admiration and respect of his equals and the confidence of his chief. He was earning £400 a year, with an unlimited expenses account, fully qualified to undertake any journalistic task the *Herald* might give him, and as likely as any man alive to bring off a scoop such as the discovery of the old explorer in the jungle. He had been in fifteen battles, three naval bombardments, and two shipwrecks,[46] and had travelled tens of thousands of miles, nearly always alone, nearly always his own master, in freezing winter and scorching heat. He was completely sure of himself, extremely capable, adaptable, and daring, absolutely without fear, and of exceptional toughness, experienced in dealing with primitive people and, above all, gifted with a resolve which nothing could break once his mind was made up. No man on Bennett's staff was more likely to succeed in such a difficult mission, no man was more able or suitable, and no one who was told about it, who knew Stanley, or had ever had anything to do with him, doubted for a moment that he was capable of it, or was in the least surprised when he triumphantly returned.

Chapter Six

STANLEY knew nothing of Africa and, except for the campaign in Abyssinia, had never been there. On the long, circuitous route which Bennett had ordered him to take before equipping the expedition at Zanzibar—Suez, Jerusalem, Constantinople, Tiflis, Teheran, Persepolis, Karachi, Bombay—a journey which in itself took over a year, he studied every book and map on the equatorial region that he could get hold of. But although the geography, climate, and inhabitants of this area had often been written about in vague and mysterious terms by geographers as long ago as Herodotus, the east and central equatorial regions were known to have been visited by Europeans only twice. The men who had done this were Richard Burton and John Speke together in 1858, and John Speke and a different companion in 1862, and their records were the only factual descriptions in existence. Burton and Speke had started from the coast opposite Zanzibar and had marched a thousand miles due west and discovered Lake Tanganyika; Speke, alone, had discovered Victoria Nyanza farther to the north, and they had returned together to Zanzibar. Fortunately for Stanley, Lake Tanganyika was the centre of the region of lakes in which Livingstone was supposed to be, and so he at least had the benefit of the experiences of Burton and Speke, who had already been there, but even their route was only a hair-thin line on an otherwise blank map of Africa, the whole centre of which was unexplored from the fringe of the Indian Ocean to the perimeter of the Atlantic, and from the Zambezi to the Sahara.

> "So geographers, in Afric-maps,
> With savage-pictures fill their gaps;
> And o'er unhabitable downs
> Place elephants for want of towns."

wrote Swift in the eighteenth century. It had been the same before this for thousands of years, and it was still to be the same
until almost the end of the Victorian era, when, as a result of the
work of Livingstone, Stanley, and many others, the equatorial
region was opened up and finally explored.

The interior had remained unknown for so long owing to its
deadly climate and almost insuperable natural barriers. The
Portuguese had sailed round the continent in the fifteenth century, but they found no easily navigable rivers and, as they
could obtain gold and slaves on the coast, they had no incen-
tive to establish themselves farther inland. No cattle or horses
could withstand the tsetse-fly and, until the use of quinine in
1850, fever was almost certain to wipe out every member of
any expedition that left the coast. The jungle itself, with its
rivers full of crocodiles, and teeming with poisonous reptiles
and dangerous wild animals and populated by hostile natives
who were often cannibals, was too unprofitable to be in the
least inviting.

It was not until nearly the end of the eighteenth century that
any organized interest in exploration was evinced, with the
formation of the African Association in 1788. This body, which
merged with the Royal Geographical Society in 1831, and
whose first president was Sir Joseph Banks, was founded for the
purpose of discovering the source and mouth of the Niger.
This was partly achieved by Mungo Park in 1805, and completed by the Lander brothers in 1830. Another step followed
in 1833 with the passing of the Emancipation Act, which
abolished slavery in the British Colonies and caused the abo-
litionists to turn their attention to the final destruction of
slavery at its source. They rightly realized that the only way to
do this was to open up and civilize the areas in which the slaves
were captured and, largely by their influence, three expeditions,
sponsored by the British Government and by private enter-
prise, went out to north-west Africa in the next twenty years
to convert the inhabitants to Christianity and to establish

trading posts. Several missionary societies, too, were operating in Africa in the first half of the nineteenth century as part of the spirit of the same movement. But the initial work of establishment of even small mission stations was extremely slow, and it was only in the eighteen sixties that even the general location of the lakes of the central region—Nyasa, Tanganyika, Albert, and Victoria—was definitely established, and another twenty years before the missionaries came there.

But although Stanley was not to be the first man to enter the great lake region, he was at least to be only the second, and it was an area of such vastness and difficulty that the only advantage in having a predecessor lay in being able to get certain advice about supplies and equipment and the indication of certain general routes and landmarks. There were no roads or recognizable tracks, and it was impossible to know more than the general line of march that had been taken by others. In any case, it would have been of no particular advantage to know this, since conditions changed, and tribal wars, floods, and seasonal weather made the precise knowledge of the route for to-morrow a matter of hazard. For anyone taking an expedition into central Africa in 1870 there was only one course, and that was to press forward and hope for the best; for it was still as unknown, wild, unpleasant, fever-ridden, remote, dangerous, and jungly as though no one had ever been there. The explorer took a blank map and filled it up as he went along, and he knew that if he got into difficulty there was only the remotest chance of anyone finding him. Although Stanley read thoroughly and took with him the books of Burton and Speke, he was frequently unable to find any resemblance to the places they mentioned.

There was not a great deal for him to learn, either, about the whereabouts of Dr. Livingstone. This famous missionary, who was now in his fifty-seventh year, and who had spent nearly the whole of his working life in Africa, was the second son of poor parents and had been born near Glasgow in 1813. At the age of ten he had been sent to work in a cotton-mill, but he had managed to educate himself in his spare time, and when he was twenty-five had succeeded in getting himself accepted as a candidate by the London Missionary Society. He had then taken a medical degree at Glasgow University and been ordained, and in 1841 had been sent out to Kuruman in Bechuanaland, the London Missionary Society's station seven hundred miles north of the Cape of Good Hope, which was under the supervision of the famous and venerable Dr. Robert Moffat. Eight years later, under the Society's orders to advance into the interior, he had begun his first long journey, crossing the Kalahari desert and travelling four hundred and fifty miles to the banks of the Zambezi near the Batoka highlands, and as a result of this expedition, two things happened to him which had a lasting influence on his career. The journey itself convinced him that his primary interest and ability lay in exploration rather than in settled missionary work, and his arrival in the Batoka highlands brought him into contact for the first time with the brutalities of the slave trade, which had just spread into this area. To these two subjects—exploration and the abolition of the slave trade—he was now to dedicate the rest of his life.

In accordance with the policy of suppression of slavery by colonization, he decided to try to establish a mission station in the Batoka highlands, and with the object of finding out the most accessible line of communication, he set off on an expedition to the Atlantic coast. This journey of well over a thousand miles, on which he was accompanied only by twenty-seven natives, took seven months, and he reached the coastal town of Loanda at the end of May 1854. As, however, the route was not suitable for general use, he returned the way he had come and continued down the Zambezi to the Indian Ocean, which he reached at Quilimane in May two years later, having thus crossed the entire continent from west to east—one of the most remarkable journeys in the history of African exploration. It was on this journey, too, that he discovered the

Victoria Falls on the Zambezi, in November 1855. Returning to England at the end of 1856, he wrote a book, "Missionary Travels and Researches in South Africa", which became a best seller. He was honoured by the Royal Geographical Society, and universally acclaimed as the outstanding African explorer of the day.

Still with the object of establishing a mission in the Batoka highlands, he now resigned from the London Missionary Society and accepted the appointment of H.M. Consul at Quilimane. With this appointment went a grant of £5,000 for the exploration of the Zambezi, and he embarked on this expedition a few months later, sailing from Liverpool in March 1858, taking with him a steam launch and being accompanied by his brother Charles and, among others, a doctor called John Kirk. Dr. Kirk, who was a young man and who joined the expedition in the capacity of botanist, became a close friend of Livingstone's, and although, fourteen years later, he was bitterly accused by Stanley of allowing Livingstone to be swindled and forgotten, he devoted his life to the destruction of the slave trade, and in that direction lived to be the principal instrument in the completion of Livingstone's work.

The Zambezi expedition, which lasted more than five years, was not generally considered a success and suffered many misfortunes, including the death of Livingstone's wife, who came out to join him and who was the daughter of his first chief, Dr. Robert Moffat. The Rev. C. F. Mackenzie, who was sent as Missionary Bishop to establish and preside over the first settlement, also died; three missionaries of his staff died too, and the whole idea of a station in the area was finally abandoned and the mission transferred to the island of Zanzibar. But there were nevertheless many important achievements, including the exploration of the Shire River and the discovery of Lake Nyasa. Livingstone returned to England in 1864, having sailed a small motor-boat with a crew of three white men and nine Africans all the way from Zanzibar to Bombay, a journey of two thousand five hundred miles. He wrote another book, "The Zambezi and its Tributaries", and the story of the discoveries and explorations it contained further increased his reputation, which had by now become world-wide.

The following year, 1865, Livingstone was asked by the President of the Royal Geographical Society—an old friend, Sir Roderick Murchison—whether he would be prepared to return to Africa to try to solve one of the principal problems still outstanding: the pattern of the watershed in the area of Lakes Nyasa and Tanganyika, and the location of the source of the Nile. Livingstone demurred at first, and suggested that Dr. Kirk might like to go, but the latter refused on the grounds that, as he hoped shortly to be married, he could not allow himself to be absent without a fixed arrangement about funds and salary—the expedition was to be financed only by grants from the Royal Geographical Society and the Government, and by public subscription. Money was not so important to Livingstone, since his books and lectures had brought him enough to live on comfortably and, learning of Kirk's position, he readily agreed to go himself. It was on this expedition that he was to disappear and be found by Stanley, an expedition which was to be his last, which was never to be completed, and on which, ultimately, he was to die.

When, in October 1869, Stanley received his instructions from Bennett, Livingstone had been absent from Europe for four years and two months. He had left England in August 1865, gone to the island of Zanzibar, where he had made his final arrangements about supplies and equipment, and had been put down on the mainland near the mouth of the river Rovuma by H.M.S. "Penguin". He travelled from choice without white companions, but he had with him sixty natives of various nationalities, three buffaloes, six camels, four donkeys, and two mules, and his plan had been first to go back to familiar ground in the area of Lake Nyasa, and then proceed north-west to Lake Tanganyika and make for a trading and fishing village called

Ujiji, a place which was well known to the Arab slave-traders and which had been visited by Burton and Speke eight years before. Being certain of the location of Ujiji, and being certain also that he would want to visit it, he arranged for various additional supplies to be sent there for his replenishment. After visiting Ujiji his plan was to cross Lake Tanganyika and explore to the west. These few facts were all that was known of his probable movements, but at the time of setting off they were quite enough, and there was no reason to suppose that he would not be able to supplement them with letters from time to time.

The first news that came, however, was brought back by a group of his own men in December 1866, who reported that he had been attacked and killed by natives near Lake Nyasa. In spite of widespread belief in this story, E. D. Young, who had been with him on the Zambezi, suggested to the Royal Geographical Society that he should lead a small party to Lake Nyasa to try to find out the truth. He reached the lake in August 1867, and quickly established that the whole report was false. To confirm this a letter from Livingstone arrived in Zanzibar in January 1868, reporting the desertion of some of his men—the same ones who had come back with the story of his death. This letter was over a year old, but it at least showed that he was not dead when he was supposed to have been; and later in the same year two more letters arrived, both also more than a year old, but both proving that he was still alive and comparatively well. These were written from an area west of Lake Mweru, in what is now the Belgian Congo, and in them Livingstone said that he had lost his medicine chest and asked for a fresh lot of medical and other supplies to be sent to Ujiji, since he planned to start out for that place in two days' time. A year later, in October 1869, a fourth letter arrived at Zanzibar saying that he had reached Ujiji in March of that year and planned next to go west to a cannibal country called Manyuema, in which there was said to be a great river which he hoped would be the Nile. If he were not eaten, he would return to Ujiji later. A summary of this letter, telegraphed from Bombay, appeared in *The Times* on the 24th of November, only three weeks after Stanley had set off from Paris. The *Herald* agent in London sent him a résumé of it, and as it agreed with all the known facts and intentions of the old explorer, there was every reason to suppose it was true.

This, then, was the position in the autumn of 1869, when Stanley received his orders: Livingstone had set off from Zanzibar into the jungle to look for the source of the Nile in March 1866, and had not been seen by white men since, but he was known three years later—in May 1869—to have been at Ujiji, on Lake Tanganyika. He was also known to have planned to go west from there to a cannibal country called Manyuema, but to return to Ujiji after exploring it, since Ujiji had been designated as his advance base, and since he had arranged that his supplies and letters should be sent there from Zanzibar.

These were the facts which were available to Stanley and on which he had to make his plans, and although there were dozens of rumours, not only of Livingstone's murder on Lake Nyasa but also of his death nearer the west coast on the upper reaches of the Congo, of his being on his way home down the Nile or, alternatively, about to appear on the Atlantic, and even of his having settled down somewhere with an African princess, perfectly content, and determined never to return to white civilization, none of these was in the least circumstantial, and Stanley quite rightly took no notice of them. He took the only obvious and safe course, and decided to go first to Ujiji. If Livingstone were not there, or had been there but had left again, Stanley would at least be certain to get fairly recent news and be able from there to start searching for him in earnest.

Chapter Seven

STANLEY arrived on the island of Zanzibar at the beginning of 1871, fifteen months after leaving Paris, having reported on the Suez Canal, inspected excavations at Jerusalem, visited the battle-fields of the Crimea, interviewed the Governor of the Caucasus at Tiflis, and made his way to the Persian Gulf via Persepolis, where he slept the night in the shadow of the monuments and cut his name on the base of one of them. From the Persian Gulf he sailed for Bombay and, after waiting there for two months for the arrival of any ship that would take him across to Africa, he finally gave up hope and made the journey in stages via Mauritius and the Seychelles—a circuit which took him another three months. It had been an interesting year, and although the work had had no bearing whatever on the Livingstone expedition, and although Bennett had never given any explanation for making him undertake it, Stanley had enjoyed it and had not wasted his time. At Jerusalem he had engaged as valet-interpreter a young Christian Arab called Selim, who had been educated at Bishop Gobat's missionary school on Mount Zion; Joy Morris, whom he had met again at Constantinople, had given him a splendid new Winchester sixteen-shot repeating rifle; at Bombay he had bought a black-and-tan Turkish watch-dog, which he christened Omar, and on the voyage from India to Mauritius on a barque called the "Polly" he had enlisted the mate, a tough-looking Scotch character called William Farquhar, to be his first lieutenant. But the waiting about at Bombay and the long, indirect journey across had exasperated him, and he had become more and more irritable and depressed as the boat from the Seychelles—an American whaler called the "Falcon"—had lain with lank sails in a glassy sea and made no progress whatever. The only excitement had been a fight one evening with the captain, an American, who had got roaring drunk and chased his wife with an axe, but as Stanley had already handled this situation once before with the judge in Brooklyn, he was not amused by it, and refused to be diverted.

But as at last, early in the morning of the 6th of January, 1871, the "Falcon" ran down into the Zanzibar Channel, Stanley went on deck and watched the sun rising over the low hills of the island, and his restless depression left him. There was a soft breeze, which ruffled the water and made it sparkle in the sunlight, the island was vivid green—far brighter and pleasanter than he had expected—with a low wooded shore and a wide strip of fine sand. Dhows with bulging sails skimmed towards them, the harbour bristled with the swaying masts of ships, while on the quay behind stood the square white blocks of the British, French, German, and American consulates, their national flags waving above them. A wispy haze that hung about the water began to lift, and as the sun rose clear above the island, Stanley suddenly tingled with excitement as he saw to the west, clearly visible in the dazzling morning air, the long, mysterious outline of the Dark Continent.

The only important thing to be done at Zanzibar was to buy certain provisions—such as flour, rice, and tinned meat—and to decide what to take in the way of beads, cloth, and brass wire, which were used as currency with the natives in the interior. This choice was difficult, since one tribe valued one kind of bead or cloth, while its neighbour would only accept something quite different. If the traveller were without the right sort of commodity he could buy nothing, and there were many things, such as milk, vegetables, and eggs, which were essential; also he could go no farther, since each tribe levied a tribute and, without the right quantity of the right goods, paid in full, he was refused permission to cross their territory. For a journey of any length this necessitated an enormous quantity of goods, which had to be carried by native porters recruited on the coast. But an expedition also had to have a guard, made up of natives of a higher quality than the porters, and these were enlisted in Zanzibar. The porters were mostly slaves or former slaves, and no man who had once been in slavery was ever very reliable, but the soldiers of the guard were free men, and among them were one or two tribal chiefs who acted as N.C.O.s.

As Stanley had pointed out to Bennett in Paris, an explorer needed a huge sum of money to do all this, and Burton and Speke's expedition was known to have cost at least three thousand pounds. When Stanley reached Zanzibar he had almost run out of money and had only sixteen pounds in gold, but he had not worried, expecting to find a draft or a cable from Bennett establishing his credit awaiting him at the American consulate. But when he went there he found there was nothing and it was obvious that, exactly as he had feared, Bennett had simply forgotten about him.

But just as he had had an exceptional piece of luck at a critical moment at New Orleans when he met his foster-father, he now had another in finding that the American Consul was still Francis Webb, to whom he had written about Livingstone two years earlier, when he had been at Aden. Webb was friendly and generous, took Stanley's word for it that he was still looking for the explorer and had now been sent to find him, and he personally guaranteed his credit to any limit. Stanley paid for everything by drafts drawn on the *Herald's* bank in New York, and although the Indian merchants would give him only seventy-five pounds for every draft of a hundred, he paid the extra without hesitation, confident that his drafts would be met,[47] and knowing that Bennett meant it when he said something was to be done regardless of cost. Webb also offered to put him up at the consulate, which was a convenience, since the only public accommodation was a villainous premises called "Charley's", and allowed him to use the consulate warehouse for baling and checking his stores, which soon lay in mountainous heaps in every direction. In the dull and restricted social life of the island, Webb would probably have welcomed Stanley as a fellow-countryman with pleasure at any time, but

he certainly would not have guaranteed his finances, especially
accounts running into thousands of pounds, if he had not
known who he was and believed the story of his appointment,
and it was a vital piece of good luck for Stanley that he did so.
For although Stanley kept the real objective of his expedition a
secret so far as the rest of the people on the island were concerned, from Webb he concealed nothing, for had he done so
he would have got no farther than Charley's bar. Not only because he would have got no money, but also because any explorer going into the interior had to rely on his country's consul
for contact with the outside world and for getting help to him
if he needed it.

In Dr. Livingstone's case this contact was naturally with the
British Consul, and Stanley went to pay a call on him soon
after his arrival to see if he could learn anything. Livingstone
was not mentioned, but Stanley was asked to an "at home" for
the following Tuesday, and decided to bring up the name himself and see if he could find out casually the latest news of his
movements. The acting consul was John Kirk, who, largely
through Livingstone's efforts, had been appointed there as
medical officer to the Political Agent; he was acting consul at
the time of Stanley's visit because the official holder of that office
was away on sick leave. As Livingstone was always a topic of
conversation at Zanzibar, and as he was an old friend of Kirk's,
Stanley thought it would be easy to talk about him without
arousing suspicion, and at the "at home" Stanley asked what he
was like and what would happen if he ran into him. But although Stanley had given out that the object of his visit to
Africa was the exploration of the Rufiji river, this river ran in an
entirely different direction from any in which Livingstone was
now supposed to be, and Kirk thought that Stanley's question
was suspicious. He did talk about Livingstone, but only in such
a way as to discourage Stanley—that Livingstone was not easy
to get on with, and that if any word reached him of a white
man in the vicinity he would put himself on the other side of a

hundred miles of swamp. Stanley felt snubbed, and when,
some days later, in Kirk's presence, he spoke of going to Ujiji,
and Kirk[48] made no sign that he welcomed the idea of anyone
going up to Livingstone's base, even though supplies and letters
might have gone up under his supervision, Stanley felt certain
that Kirk was doing his best to put him off. This was probably
so, but Kirk was a punctilious servant of the Government, and
there was something odd about someone who claimed to be an
American newspaper-man suddenly turning up on the island
and spending gigantic amounts of money for the apparent purpose of exploring an insignificant river, and Kirk behaved, as it
was his duty to do, with official reserve until he saw what
Stanley was doing. Commercial relations between America
and Britain were somewhat strained at that time in the area,
and Stanley might be up to no good. It has been said that if Kirk
had known that Stanley was actually going to Ujiji, he would
have done everything he could for him, being as anxious as
anyone else that supplies for Livingstone should be got there as
quickly as possible. This is not the case; he did know, but he
chose to do nothing about it for reasons which he considered
justified. But to Stanley, already excited and anxious about the
welfare of the old explorer, Kirk's outlook was merely one of
indifference, and this was confirmed in Stanley's view by the
discovery three weeks later that the latest supply column for
Livingstone had been loitering about on the coast opposite at
Bagamoyo for three months waiting for porters, and was still
there until ten days before he left himself. Kirk had failed to
check on this caravan to see if it had got away, but he had been
ill and doing the work of two men. "My hand starts and shakes
and my head is giddy," he had written to Livingstone in a
letter [49] which went with this column, and he could not be
blamed altogether. But Stanley felt it was inexcusable, and lost
no time in saying so to Livingstone when he met him. To Stanley, Kirk appeared just another supercilious Britisher, a type of
man from whom he had already suffered more than enough,

and from that moment he never missed a chance of attacking him in the *Herald* and of speaking of him with scorn.

But apart from his rebuff by Kirk, everything went according to plan and, accumulating stores and equipment with a furious energy, by the end of the month Stanley had assembled, baled, and crated everything he wanted. He had enlisted another white man to be co-lieutenant with Farquhar—an Englishman called John Shaw—and had recruited a company of native guards under the sergeant-majorship[50] of a burly negro called Bombay, who had already been to Ujiji with Burton and Speke. Stanley borrowed a top hat from Webb and called on the Sultan of Zanzibar, who gave him letters of recommendation to his Arab agents in the interior, and under a gaily waving representation of the Stars and Stripes which had been made for him by Mrs. Webb, the whole party set sail for Bagamoyo on the 5th of February.

In six weeks Stanley found the porters he needed, and he was ready to leave at last. He dined with Father Horner at the French Mission,[51] and was regaled with excellent wine and the singing of a melodious choir of native schoolchildren. He hoped he would not be away for much longer than a year, and unless he had to follow Livingstone right across to the Atlantic, he thought he might get back to Bagamoyo a good deal sooner. But Father Horner, a veteran missionary of eighteen years' experience of the East African climate, must have looked at Stanley's round, red, animated face and wondered if he would ever see it again.

The expedition was provisioned for two years and set off in five contingents at different times between the 18th of February and the 21st of March, one party under command of Farquhar, three others under tribal headmen who acted as sergeants, and the fifth under command of Shaw. In addition to Farquhar, Shaw, Stanley, a gun-bearer, and the interpreter, Selim, there was a cook, a carpenter and a tailor, three sergeants and Bombay, the sergeant-major, a guard of twenty-three men, and one hundred and fifty-seven porters—a total, in all, of one hundred and ninety-two persons; there were also two horses, twenty-seven donkeys, the watch-dog, Omar, and some goats.

Farquhar, having been engaged first, was treated as the senior lieutenant, although both he and Shaw had the same wages of £60 a year;[52] Bombay had £16 a year; the soldiers had £7 4s. a year, and the porters, who would only hire themselves to the trading-post of Tabora—a place two-thirds of the way between the coast and Ujiji—each had a down payment of £2 8s. Each donkey cost around £4, and each goat about 8s.

For weapons[53] the expedition carried two "sixteen shooters" (one Winchester, one Henry), three single-shot breech-loading rifles (two Starr's, one Jocelyn), one elephant rifle, and one double-barrelled breech-loading smooth-bore gun. Also two breech-loading revolvers, twenty-four flintlock muskets, and six single-barrelled pistols; one battle-axe, two swords, two Persian daggers, one boar-spear, two American 4-lb. axes, twenty-four hatchets, and twenty-four butcher's knives.

For tribute,[54] and to buy food, Stanley took sixteen thousand yards of 30-inch American unbleached calico at 6d. a yard, eight thousand yards of light-weight Indian blue jeans at 3d. a yard, and five thousand two hundred yards of finer blue and pink muslins and crimson broadcloth at different prices up to 6d. a yard—total length of material 19¼ miles. He also took over a million beads (thirty-six thousand five hundred necklaces) of eleven different sorts and colours at 6d. to 1s. a pound. They were made of coral, glass, or china, some as big as marbles, others as small as seed-pearls, and of all different colours and mixtures of colours—black, brick, dove-grey, coral pink, vitreous blue, transparent palm-leaf green. In addition he took with him three hundred and fifty pounds of No. 5 and No. 6 gauge brass wire at 1s. per pound.

All this was baled into eighty-two loads of 72 lb. each, 72 lb. being the standard weight for one porter, and half the normal load for a donkey. There were also seventy-one cases of ammunition, candles, soap, pots and pans, Mocha coffee, tea, sugar, flour, rice, sardines, pemmican, and Leibig's extract of meat; and three tents, two collapsed boats, and a bath. The total weight was nearly six tons, and the cost more than four thousand pounds [55]—equivalent to sixteen thousand pounds to-day.

Stanley's personal belongings, which he carried in square leather trunks, included a camp bed, a hammock, a bearskin (for a blanket), a Persian carpet, a table, plates and cups and saucers, knives and forks, silver spoons, a silver teapot, two silver goblets, and a bottle of Sillery [56] champagne for the day when he met Livingstone. His accoutrements included field-glasses, a sextant, a pocket compass, one hundred and fifteen fathoms of sounding line, a bull's-eye lantern, a dog whip, and a meer-schaum pipe. He had a medicine chest, in which were quinine, concentrated ammonia, Dover's powder, Collis Browne's Chlorodyne, a bottle of Elixir Vegetal de la Grande Chartreuse, and a "little medical book", while for reading matter he had the Bible and bundles of back numbers of the *New York Herald*. He had also a certain amount of cash in gold.

In Africa a caravan had to make three starts before it really got going: a little start, a great start, and a final start, each start representing a journey of increasing length and each one taking a day. The last party under Shaw got off to the little start on the 21st of March, and Stanley went with it; Shaw, in sea-boots and a topee like a canoe, riding in the rear on a donkey, and Stanley, in a "Hawkes patent cork solar topee", white flannel tunic and trousers, and Wellington boots, riding at the head on a splendid bay horse—a present from an American at Zanzibar. He led the other horse, which was a grey Arab, the gift of the Sultan, and at its heels trotted his watch-dog, Omar.

"The vanguard, the reporter, the thinker, and leader of the Expedition," he described himself.

"We left Bagamoyo the attraction of all the curious, with much *éclat*, and defiled up a narrow lane shaded almost to twilight by the dense umbrage of two parallel hedges of mimosas. We were all in the highest spirits. The soldiers sang, the Kirangozi (guide) lifted his voice into a loud bellowing note, and fluttered the American flag, which told all on-lookers, 'Lo, a Musungu's (white man's) caravan!' and my heart, I thought, palpitated much too quickly for the sober face of a leader. But I could not check it; the enthusiasm of youth still clung to me—despite my travels; my pulses bounded with the full glow of staple health; behind me were the troubles which had harassed me for over two months . . . before me beamed the sun of promise as he sped towards the Occident. Loveliness glowed around me. I saw fertile fields, riant vegetation, strange trees—I heard the cry of cricket and pee-wit, and the sibilant sound of many insects, all of which seemed to tell me, 'At last you are started.' What could I do but lift my face toward the pure-glowing sky, and cry, 'God be thanked!' " [57]

The route to Ujiji lay almost due west for seven hundred and forty-two miles, first through dense level coastal jungle and then up four thousand feet over the Usagara range on to the central plateau, which stretched for almost six hundred miles through the Mountains of the Moon to the banks of the Tanganyika. Arab traders had used this route for a hundred years, carrying up cloth and beads and returning with slaves and ivory, each year pushing farther and farther afield, and reaching Ujiji in 1841, where they established a colony and built a port. Generations of caravans had made tracks, padded to the hardness of brick by the countless feet of the slaves and porters, and these tracks were easily recognizable to native guides, but in many places they were no more than nine inches wide, and the sharp thorns and cacti of the undergrowth tore at the traveller as he passed.

Two hundred and twelve miles from the coast the Arabs had established another colony at Tabora in 1820, where many of them had elaborate houses and lived in luxury. There were no other Arab settlements on this route between Tabora and Bagamoyo, but there were native villages of all sizes and two native townships, Mpwapwa and Simbamwenni, one hundred and eighty-seven and one hundred and nineteen miles from the coast respectively, and at these caravans could rest safely and buy plenty of food and get good water.

Over its whole length the route passed through the territory of thirteen different tribes, whose characters varied from friendly, to suspicious, to fierce and grasping, and with many of them not only the chiefs demanded tribute, but all their henchmen as well. Much of the scenery was superb. There were gigantic, mist-wrapped ranges of mountains below which the deep green ocean of the jungle stretched away into the hazy distance; vast, undulating parkland full of game and shady trees and clear streams. There were lion, giraffe, elephant, wild boar, and dazzling herds of hartebeest and zebra. But the jungle was infested with every conceivable bug, snake, ant, and beetle, and swarming with mosquito and tsetse. Malaria and dysentery were inevitable, in the brightest sunlight the paths through the jungle were dark and reeked with foul miasmas, and bandits shadowed the caravans and pounced on stragglers, robbing them and torturing them to death.[58]

There is still no direct highway along this route, but by 1914 both Ujiji and Tabora were directly connected by rail to Dar-es-Salaam, thirty-six miles south of Zanzibar. Tabora has become an important town with an airport, the headquarters of the Western Province, but with the enforced suppression of the slave trade in the 1870's Ujiji declined, and is now only a native fishing village in the ruins of the old Arab port, and the railway terminates three miles north, at Kigoma.

The first halting-place—Simbamwenni, the "City of the Lion"—was a fortified native township of four or five thousand inhabitants, ruled over by the daughter of a bandit, and Stanley reached it successfully after twenty-nine days, on the

17th of April. Although two Arab caravans ahead of him had both done the whole distance in eight days, he was satisfied with the way things had gone and was in good spirits, for his men had settled down and he had established an absolute discipline over them. The baling and loading had proved satisfactory and he had successfully dealt with the first of the native chiefs who had tried to obstruct him. He had gained important experience of general conditions, and with the increasing distance from civilization he had felt more calm and clear in his purpose and more certain of its worth and success. Best of all, the day before he arrived he had met an Arab caravan from the interior with direct news of Livingstone. The Arab had seen him at Ujiji and had lived in the next hut to him for a fortnight, and described him as looking old, with a long grey beard and moustaches, just recovered from a severe illness, and about to visit a country called Manyuema on the other side of the lake.

Stanley and his party rested at Simbamwenni for five days—he had intended to stop for two, but was held up by the torrential rain of the rainy season, which was in full swing. He then pressed on to the next place—Mpwapwa, sixty-eight miles farther—which he reached exactly a month later, on the 17th of May. He was now going as fast as any experienced traveller. Just before Simbamwenni he had caught up his own fourth caravan, which had repeatedly lagged behind and held him up. At Simbamwenni he again sent it on ahead, and from then on it managed to keep in front. But on the 9th of May he overtook the third party, commanded by Farquhar, which he found in a chaotic state, and Farquhar himself swollen with elephantiasis and unable to move. Farquhar had given or bartered away sixteen out of the eighteen bales of merchandise of his caravan to buy luxury food for himself, such as chickens, he had killed nine of his ten donkeys from overwork, and had cursed and beaten his followers into a state of incapability and hysteria.

Shaw had been under supervision, since Stanley was travelling with him, but he, too, had turned out unsatisfactorily—a sullen, whimpering brute, not much better or more capable than Farquhar; he, too, had been sick, with a lingering attack of ague; he had completely given way to it, and behaved like a fractious old woman. In this mood he and Farquhar formed a dangerous combination, and by the end of a week they were determined to make trouble.

Early in the morning of the 15th of May Stanley noticed Farquhar and Shaw whispering together suspiciously. They came to his tent for breakfast as usual, and he asked them to take their places, and called out to Selim to bring the meal. There was roast quarter of goat, stewed liver, half a dozen sweet potatoes, hot pancakes, and coffee. Stanley asked Shaw to carve, but instead of doing so, Shaw looked at the joint and inquired insolently what kind of dog's meat it was they were having thrown at them on this occasion. Stanley asked him what he meant by such a remark, and Shaw jumped up and told him with a stream of abuse exactly what he meant: that he would rather be in hell than with the *Herald* Expedition, and that he wished the whole party at the bottom of the sea. He would have said more, but Stanley knocked him down, and Shaw, climbing to his feet, merely finished by saying he would like to be discharged and allowed to go back to Zanzibar immediately.

Stanley agreed to this without hesitation, and called for Bombay to collect Shaw's gun and pistol and to strike his tent and take him, the tent, and all his belongings two hundred yards outside the camp and leave them there. This was done.

After a few minutes Bombay came back to Stanley and said that Shaw wanted to speak to him. Stanley went out, and found Shaw at the entrance to the camp, begging to be forgiven and allowed back. Stanley shook his hand and told him not to mention it, and that so far as he was concerned the matter was closed.

But late that night, as Stanley was lying in bed, there was a shot, and a bullet ripped through his tent, just above his body.

He jumped up and ran out to the watchmen. They pointed to Shaw's tent. He lit a candle and walked across to it.

Shaw was breathing heavily, pretending to be asleep, and when Stanley asked him if he had fired, he opened his eyes and said he had been dreaming. Stanley noticed his gun beside him, and bending down and touching the end of it, found it warm and his finger blackened with powder.

"What is this?" he asked, holding up his finger.

Shaw said he remembered, after all: he had dreamt of a thief passing his tent and had taken a shot at him; was anything the matter?

Stanley said nothing was the matter, but Shaw had better take more care in future not to shoot so close to his tent, or he might get hurt, and that would cause unfortunate rumours. He said good-night, and went back to bed.

Apart from this incident, nothing very exciting had happened up to this point, and the worst experience Stanley had suffered was when he had gone out hunting alone one day when the expedition was resting, and had got lost. He had found himself in such thick undergrowth that he had to crawl back to camp on his hands and knees, steering by compass, and being dressed only in a topee, flannel pyjamas, and canvas shoes, he had got terribly torn in the process. Writing about it in "How I Found Livingstone", and expanding himself in heavy prose, he described it as causing "ruthless rents and epidermal wounds, ruinous to clothes and trying to the cuticle". He swore he would never leave camp again without a guide.

But the most difficult thing of all during the first two months had been simply to keep going. With typical disregard of everything in his way, he had set off against local advice only two days before the rainy season, which lasted for thirty-nine days. Every item of equipment had often to be dried, cleaned, and greased at the end of every day. Small streams became torrents over which he had to build bridges and through which he had to lead the donkeys, having to unload their packs and carry them over separately. Sometimes this had to be done five times a day, and on two occasions one river alone took five hours to cross. The valley of the Makata river, through which he had to pass at this time, flooded into a swamp thirty miles wide, with water up to five feet deep, through which he had to whip his bearers and donkeys for eight days. The donkeys died by twos and threes and, as well as Shaw and Farquhar, many of the men fell sick, and he himself had attacks both of ague and acute dysentery.

On the coast the temperature had been no more than 85°, but in some places inland it had reached 128°.

The bugs, too, had been frightful: armies of black, white, and red ants, centipedes like worms, wasps with stings like scorpions, earwigs by the hundreds of thousands, beetles as large as mice.

By the time they arrived at Mpwapwa, Farquhar was too sick to go farther, two of the bearers had died, one had deserted, the cook had run away after being whipped for stealing, and many of the other bearers were ill and weak from dysentery contracted in the swamp. Only ten donkeys were left out of twenty-seven, and four of these were so weak that they were useless, both the horses had died, and also the watch-dog. But Stanley was cheerful and happy, and content to have got on as well as he had.

"Thank God!" he wrote in his diary on the evening of the first day after his arrival at Mpwapwa. "After fifty-seven days of living on matama porridge and tough goat, I have enjoyed with unctuous satisfaction a real breakfast and dinner."

Mpwapwa he described with derision. The natives were timid. It was just the place to establish a mission!

On the 22nd of May, after five days' rest, Stanley set off again, accompanied by two other caravans belonging to Arab merchants. He had managed to pick up twelve good porters, which to some extent made up for the loss of the donkeys, and he was no longer encumbered by Farquhar, whom he had left behind with an interpreter and six months' rations. Altogether the three caravans numbered about four hundred men.

The route lay through the territory of a conceited and grasping people called the Wagogo, to whose eight regional chiefs all caravans had to pay tribute in cloth and beads, and sometimes, between them, Stanley and the Arabs had to pay as much as £10.

Before the land of the Wagogo there was a scorching, waterless desert thirty miles wide which had to be crossed by forced marches. A third of the way across, Stanley had an attack of fever, and as it was impossible to stop, he had to be carried. By the time they reached the other side, after marching for thirty hours with only one halt, he had recovered, but the fever never completely left him, and for the next three weeks he was repeatedly prostrated by it.

On the other side of the Wagogo lay the Land of the Moon, an uninhabited wilderness with water only at wide intervals which also had to be crossed by forced marches. At one point there was a choice of routes, and when Stanley ordered the most difficult because, typically, it was the shortest, his porters threw down their loads and refused to go on. He immediately ordered his soldiers to flank the caravan and shoot the first man who moved, and, seizing his dog-whip, threatened to flog anyone who did not pick up his bale instantly. By his quickness he avoided trouble, and the men took up their loads and marched on.

On one day they marched eighteen and three-quarter miles without a halt, and on another day twenty miles, and they travelled the whole of the last hundred and seventy-eight miles in sixteen days, including pauses.

He lost two more bearers, one from weakness and one from smallpox, and six more donkeys, and he himself had six further attacks of fever. But they arrived safely and triumphantly at Tabora on the 23rd of June with the Stars and Stripes flying, and blasts of horns, and shouts and songs and fusillades, the men marching as briskly as the day they started, glorious in new loincloths and clean white shirts. The first, second, and fourth caravans had all arrived safely ahead of them, and Stanley bought a bullock and ordered a feast. Tabora was five hundred and twenty-five miles from the coast, and the journey had taken three months and two days.

Between the coast and Tabora he had lost two soldiers and eight bearers, twenty-five donkeys, both horses, and the dog. One of his lieutenants had dropped out and the other had proved a mutinous hypochondriac. He himself had had seven attacks of fever and one of dysentery.

But he was now thoroughly settled, experienced, and sure of himself, and certain that if Livingstone were to be found, he would reach him. The isolation and solitude of the last three months had made the hurly-burly of his past life and the wranglings and agitation of the outside world seem stupid and unimportant. As he had lain in his tent at night, reading the Bible, much of the religious conviction of his Nonconformist Welsh childhood had come back to him. He had begun to feel himself on a mission, divinely directed, the relief of Livingstone a task for which he had been chosen, and to which he must give himself completely. He prophesied that the men of his party would be crowned as Immortals, and he meant it, and he saw no reason why they should not be. Just before leaving Tabora for the next and last lap of the journey he wrote in his diary:

". . . I have taken a solemn, enduring oath, an oath to be kept while the least hope of life remains in me, not to be tempted to break the resolution I have formed, never to give up the search, until I find Livingstone alive, or find his dead body; and never to return home without the strongest possible proofs that he is alive, or that he is dead. No living man, or living men, shall stop me, only death can prevent me. But death—not even this; I shall not die, I will not die,

I cannot die! And something tells me, I do not know what it is—perhaps it is the ever-living hopefulness of my own nature, perhaps it is natural presumption born out of an abundant and glowing vitality, or the outcome of an overweening confidence in one's self—anyhow and everyhow, something tells me to-night I shall find him, and—write it larger—FIND HIM! FIND HIM! Even the words are inspiring. I feel more happy. Have I uttered a prayer? I shall sleep calmly to-night." [59]

Chapter Eight

As the first, second, and fourth caravans had already arrived, Stanley was expected at Tabora and the Arab sheikhs came out and welcomed him warmly. He was offered a fine encampment about a mile south-west of the Arab compound, and was given presents of oxen, sheep, goats, chickens, eggs, and huge plates of cooked rice, vegetables, and fruit. He was invited over to the Arab encampment for a feast in his honour, and three days later he marched over for it with Selim and an escort of eighteen brightly dressed men.

On his arrival at Tabora he had found that the road to Ujiji was blocked by a bandit chief, Mirambo—the "African Bonaparte"—who had sworn that no caravan should get through without his permission and that unless the Arabs supported him against his enemies he would attack Tabora and wipe it out. Before the feast there was a council of war, and it was decided to send an expedition to try to trap Mirambo at a village where he was thought to be, about thirty miles off. Stanley heartily supported this and said that he would take part in it.

The porters originally hired on the coast had left him, according to contract, but some of them joined up again, and by the end of the month he had assembled a new contingent of fifty men. On the 29th of July they set off with great swagger to meet the Arab army, which had gone ahead. They were fully equipped for the final march to Ujiji, and Stanley planned to dump his stores under a few guards a little way back during the battle and to collect them and march on, after it was won.

"Hoy! hoy!" shouted the giant leader of the party who carried the Stars and Stripes.

"Hoy! hoy!" answered the men.

"Where are ye going?"

"Going to war."

"Against whom?"
"Against Mirambo."
"Who is your master?"
"The White Man."
"Ough! ough!"
"Ough! ough!"
"Hyah! hyah!"
"Hyah! hyah!" [60]

At the end of three days they overtook the Arabs, and two days later they attacked Mirambo's village and occupied it, although Mirambo escaped with his son and most of his men. But after another two days Mirambo ambushed and massacred a company of five hundred Arabs as they were returning to camp, encumbered with loot and three hundred slaves whom they had just captured in another village. When word of this disaster reached the rest of the Arab army there was panic and in a few minutes the whole force had fled and disappeared into the jungle.

When the news came Stanley was in bed with fever and could hardly move. He got up to find that all the Arab leaders had deserted him, and all but seven of his own men had run away, and as he reached the door of his tent he saw Shaw frantically getting ready a donkey on to which he was buckling Stanley's own saddle. Shaw had developed syphilis and had become so feeble-minded that Stanley had ceased to pay much attention to him, and on this occasion he only forced him to get his own harness and ride with him as hard as he could, held up by natives on both sides when he refused to go on. Stanley was in great pain himself and could hardly keep his seat, but he was determined that if he could do it, Shaw should do so too. He had warned the Arabs against ambush, and was furious with them for their stupidity and cowardly selfishness in deserting him, and he swore that when he got back to Tabora he would have nothing further to do with them.

At the end of August Mirambo attacked Tabora and burnt it

to the ground. Stanley's camp was far enough away to escape, and although he was asked for help by the Arabs, he refused, and instead fortified his own enclosure as quickly as he could and settled down for a siege. But he realized now that if he did nothing, with Mirambo in control of the route to the west he might have to wait for years before he could get through, so he set about organizing a flying column to break out and try to reach Ujiji by a detour to the south.

Stanley had again had news of Livingstone. He was told by a man that after Livingstone had recovered from his illness he had gone west to Manyuema, as the Arab merchant whom Stanley had met earlier had said he would. Livingstone had been on foot, dressed in a cap and American sheeting, and had lost all his bales in a canoe which capsized in a lake; he was carrying two revolvers and a double-barrelled rifle, and had been deserted by several of his men. If it were true about the loss of the cloth, it was a disaster, because without it he might not even be able to get enough food to enable him to get back to Ujiji.

During the three months that Stanley was at Tabora he received word that Farquhar had died. Farquhar had got up one day, saying that he was fit enough to leave, and had fallen down dead. His body had been dragged into the jungle and left there naked.

"There is one of us gone, Shaw my boy! Who will be the next?" Stanley exclaimed when he heard it.

Shaw, who was very sick by this time, probably did not think this funny. But although he had tried to murder Stanley and also to desert him and leave him to be captured by Mirambo, Stanley continued to look after him with compassionate and fatherly gentleness, realizing that much of the time he was too ill to know what he was doing.

Three soldiers were sent to Zanzibar for special medicine, and Stanley promised them £10 each if they got back quickly telling them to report to Dr. Christie, the Sultan's physician.

In a letter to Christie, Stanley gave a list of the various items he
needed and begged him to do all he could to send them at once
and not to hold them up for lack of money. He promised to be
back in Zanzibar in six months,[61] when he would repay any
loan with interest, and as an interim payment he enclosed £6 in
gold. He wrote also to the American Consul, Webb, giving an
account of the war with Mirambo and the cutting of the road
to Ujiji, and he also sent a despatch to the *New York Herald*
which gave the first news of his mission. In the meantime he
petted and pampered Shaw, cooked for him, sat with him, and
talked to him like a nannie. He tried to cheer him up by telling
him that the real point of going to Ujiji was to find Dr. Livingstone, and that if they succeeded, the *New York Herald* would
give them enough money to last for the rest of their lives. This
did not stimulate Shaw at all. Stanley made him some punch
with eggs, sugar, lemon and spice, and begged him to take it.
Shaw paid no attention, and Stanley was exasperated and
longed to give him a good beating.

But soon after they arrived at Tabora, Stanley himself became very ill, too.

> "On the 7th of July, about 2 p.m., I was sitting on the
> burzani (verandah) as usual; I felt listless and languid, and a
> drowsiness came over me; I did not fall asleep, but the power
> of my limbs seemed to fail me. Yet the brain was busy; all
> my life seemed passing in review before me; when these re-
> trospective scenes became serious, I looked serious; when
> they were sorrowful, I wept hysterically; when they were
> joyous, I laughed loudly. Reminiscences of a yet young life's
> battles and hard struggles came surging into the mind in
> quick succession; events of boyhood, of youth, and man-
> hood; perils, travels, scenes, joys, and sorrows; loves and
> hates; friendships and indifferences. My mind followed the
> various and rapid transition of my life's passages; it drew the
> lengthy, erratic, sinuous lines of travel my footsteps had

passed over. If I had drawn them on the sandy floor, what enigmatical problems they had been to those around me, and what plain, readable, intelligent histories they had been to me!

"The loveliest feature of all to me was the form of a noble, and true man, who called me son. Of my life in the great pine forests of Arkansas, and in Missouri, I retained the most vivid impressions. The dreaming days I passed under the sighing pines on the Ouachita's shores; the new clearing, the block-house, our faithful black servant, the forest deer, and the exuberant life I led, were all well remembered. And I remembered how one day, after we had come to live near the Mississippi, I floated down, down, hundreds of miles, with a wild fraternity of knurly giants, the boatmen of the Mississippi, and how a dear old man welcomed me back, as if from the grave. I remembered also my travels on foot through sunny Spain, and France, with numberless adventures in Asia Minor, among Kurdish nomads. I remembered the battle-fields of America and the stormy scenes of rampant war. I remembered gold mines, and broad prairies, Indian councils, and much experience in the new western lands. I remembered the shock it gave me to hear after my return from a barbarous country of the calamity that had overtaken the fond man whom I called father, and the hot fitful life that followed it. Stop!****** Dear me; is it the 21st of July? Yes, Shaw informed me that it was the 21st of July after I recovered from my terrible attack of fever; the true date was the 14th of July, but I was not aware that I had jumped a week until I met Dr. Livingstone." [62]

Only two other events of interest took place while he was at Tabora, one of which was the gift from an Arab of a little seven-year-old native boy whom he christened Kalulu—fawn —because of his bright eyes and slim body, and the other, the making of a joint camp with the relief caravan for Livingstone, the one which had been hanging about at Bagamoyo while he himself had been recruiting porters there. The thirty-three men of this party had reached Tabora four weeks ahead of him and had reported to the chief Sheikh of Tabora, who was the agent of the British Consul at Zanzibar, and at Stanley's suggestion they came and lived with his men and stored their goods in his enclosure. But although he was given a packet of letters for Livingstone when he left, he was not allowed by the Sheikh to take on to Ujiji any of the supplies, and he had, of course, no authority or responsibility to do so.

Before he left in September he wrote this report to the New York Herald:

"I have been in Unyanyembe (Tabora) close on three months now. By and by I shall tell you why; but first I should like to give you a glimpse of our life here. The Herald Expedition has its quarters in a large, strong house, built of mud, with walls three feet thick.[63] It is of one storey, with a broad mud verandah in front, and a broad flat roof. The great door [64] is situated directly in the centre of the front, and is the only one possible means of ingress and egress. Entering in at this door, we find a roomy hall-way; on our right is the strong store-room, where the goods of the Herald Expedition and Livingstone's caravan are kept well padlocked up, to guard against burglars.

"Soldiers at night occupy this hall-way with loaded guns, and during the day, there are always two men on guard, besides Burton's bull-headed Mabrouki,[65] who acts as my porter or policeman. On our left is a room open to the hallway, on the floor of which are spread straw mats, and two or three Persian carpets, where the Arab sheikhs squat, when they come to visit me. Passing through the hall-way, we come to the court-yard, a large quadrangle, fenced in and built around with houses. There are about a dozen pomegranate trees planted in the yard, more for their shade than for their fruit.

"The houses around consist, first, of the grainery, where we keep the rice, the matama, the Indian corn, the sweet potatoes, etc.; next comes the very much besmoked kitchen a primitive affair, merely a few stones on which the pots are placed. The cook and his youthful subs are protected from the influences of the weather by a shed. Next to the kitchen is the stable, where the few remaining animals of the expedition are housed at night. These are two donkeys, one milch cow, and six milch goats. The cow and the goats furnish me with milk for my gruel, my puddings, my sauces, and my tea. (I was obliged to attend to my comfort, and make use of the best African offers.)

"Next to the stable is another large shed, which serves as a barracks for the soldiers. Here they stow themselves and their wives, their pots and beds, and find it pretty comfortable. Next to this is the house of the white man, my nautical help, where he can be just as exclusive as he likes, has his own bedroom, verandah, bathroom, etc.; his tent serves him for a curtain, and, in English phrase, he has often declared it to be 'jolly and no mistake'.

"Occupying the half of one side of the house are my quarters, said quarters consisting of two well-plastered and neat rooms. My table is an ox-hide stretched over a wooden frame. Two portmanteaux, one on top of the other, serve for a chair. My bedstead is only a duplicate of my table, over which I spread my bearskin and Persian carpet.

"When the very greatest and most important of the Arab sheikhs visit me, Selim, my invaluable adjunct, is always told to fetch the bearskin and Persian carpet from the bed. Recesses in the solid wall answer for shelves and cupboards, where I deposit my cream-pots, and butter, and cheese (which I make myself), and my one bottle of Worcestershire sauce, and my tin candle-stick. Behind this room, which is the bed, reception, sitting, drawing room, office, pantry, etc. is my bath-room where are my saddle, my guns and ammunition always ready, my tools, and the one hundred little things which an expedition into the country must have. Adjoining my quarters is the jail of the fortlet, called 'tembe' here—a small room, eight by six feet, lit up by a small air hole, just large enough to put a rifle through—where my incorrigibles are kept for forty hours, without food, in solitary confinement. This solitary confinement answers admirably, about as well as being chained when on the road, and much better than a brutal flogging.

"In the early morning, generally about half-past five or six o'clock, I begin to stir the soldiers up, sometimes with a long bamboo, for you know they are such hard sleepers they require a good deal of poking. Bombay has his orders given him, and Feragji, the cook, who long ago warned by the noise I make when I rouse up, is told in unmistaken tones, to bring 'chai' (tea), for I am like an old woman, I love tea very much, and can take a quart and a half without any inconvenience.

"If I have any calls to make, this is generally the hour; if there are none to make, I go on the piazza and subside quietly on my bearskin to dream, may be, of that far off land I call my own. . . . But dreaming and wondering, and thinking and marvelling, are too hard for me; this constitution of mine is not able to stand it; so I make some ethnological notes, and polish up a little my geographical knowledge of Central Africa.

"I have to greet about four hundred and ninety-nine people of all sorts, with the salutation 'Yambo'.

"Having disposed of my usual number of 'Yambos' for the morning, I begin to feel 'peckish', as the sea skipper says, and Feragji, the cook, and the youthful Kalulu, the chief butler, are again called and told to bring 'chukula'—food. This is the breakfast put down on the table at the hour of ten punctually every morning:— Tea, ugali (a native porridge), . . . a dish of rice and curry.

"After breakfast the soldiers are called, and together we begin to pack the bales of cloth, string the beads and apportion the several loads, which the escort must carry to Ujiji some way or another.

"It is now the dinner hour, seven p.m.; Feragji has spread himself out, as they say. He has all sorts of little fixings ready, such as indigestible dampers, the everlasting ugali, or porridge, the sweet potatoes, chicken and roast quarter of a goat; and lastly, a custard, or something just as good, made out of plantains.

"At eight p.m. the table is cleared, the candles are lit, pipes are brought out, and Shaw, my white man, is invited to talk. But poor Shaw is sick and has not a grain of spirit or energy left in him. All I can do or say does not cheer him up in the least. He hangs down his head, and with many a sigh declares his inability to proceed with me to Ujiji."

Chapter Nine

AFTER the defeat by Mirambo, Stanley had only thirteen men left. He decided to engage fifty men to form a flying caravan and try to break out and outflank Mirambo, and at the end of August he began to recruit them at treble hire to carry loads of 50 lb.—20 lb. lighter than normal. He still had over three and a half tons of stores, and he decided to leave most of them behind under a few guards and hope for the best. For his own equipment he allowed himself only one small portmanteau.

At the end of four weeks he had got hold of fifty-four men, some local, some of them his original porters from the coast and some who lived at Ujiji and wanted to get home. On the 17th of September he gave a farewell banquet of two bullocks, three sheep, two goats, fifteen chickens, one hundred and twenty pounds of rice, twenty large loaves of corn bread, a hundred eggs, ten pounds of butter, and five gallons of milk. Afterwards there was a dance, for which he provided local beer in five-gallon jars, and all the men came to it, and brought over one hundred wives and children and friends. He meant to leave two days later, on the 19th, but he had a slight attack of fever and was delayed for twenty-four hours. At the end of that time, although still weak, he felt strong enough to go, and despite the warnings of the Arabs and lack of enthusiasm of Shaw, he roused the men early in the morning and ordered them to get ready, striding about the sleeping camp cracking his whip in the air.

He was excited as he paraded them outside his hut and counted them. "These are the men and boys whom I had selected to be crowned as Immortals . . ." he wrote proudly as he listed them in his diary. Ujiji was only a month's march by direct route, and even with a wide detour it ought not to take much longer.

As usual, a large crowd gathered to see them off, and the Arab chiefs came to wish him luck and shake their heads at his foolishness. He would die on the route and never be seen again. But this sort of gloom only annoyed him and made him all the more determined to get on. He had said he would leave on the 20th, and he refused to change his mind again.

The expedition was eventually all present except for Bombay, who was at last found in the arms of his mistress. He answered insolently when Stanley asked him why he was late, and Stanley, who was thoroughly irritated already by the jeremiads of the sheikhs on top of all the usual delays, lashed at him with his dog-whip. The Arabs wailed in affected pity, which made him angrier than ever, but Bombay soon became penitent and took his place in front of the men. The order to march was given, the flags were unfurled, the loads taken up, and with the usual shouts, songs, and explosions of firearms, the caravan set off.

Stanley shook hands with the Arabs and turned to Shaw and ordered him to mount his donkey and carry on. Shaw hung back, begged to be excused, said he was ill, that he must be left behind, but Stanley told him not to make a fuss and ordered Selim and Bombay to help him up. As the last man left the enclosure Stanley looked back and raised his hat in farewell to the Arabs. As he did so, one of the men jabbed a stick into the rump of Shaw's donkey, and it sprang into the air and threw him to the ground under a bush. Shaw screamed and lay where he had fallen, and when Stanley came up to see what was the matter, Shaw implored him to let him remain in Tabora, but Stanley firmly ordered him to get up, and helped him on to his donkey, and they marched on. But during the next week Shaw fell off so often and lay making such a fuss until he was picked up, that at last, when he tumbled off for the twentieth time, Stanley ordered him to be left, and he lay for a full hour in the blazing sun, crying like a baby. Stanley reasoned with him, but it was no use, and he finally decided to let him have his way and send him back.

That evening Shaw sat with Stanley in his tent and played an accordion which Stanley had given him at Zanzibar. As the reedy notes sank into the whirring tropical night they sounded like angelic harmonies, and when Shaw for the last time played "Home Sweet Home", both men felt very upset. Stanley was easily moved by occasions of this kind, and for two pins he could have taken Shaw by the arms and cried over his shoulder. The next morning Shaw was carried back to camp on a litter by four strong men, provisioned with some bread and a canteen of cold tea and a roast leg of kid. No European was ever to see him again, and he was to have the doubtful distinction of being the first white man to die at Tabora.

At this point, the 27th of September, Stanley also discarded all the others who were weak or unwilling and left them under medical care or let them go back. The caravan had been on the road for a week and had settled down well, and from this halt the march got going in earnest.

From now on the forest opened out into a magnificent rolling grassy plain and there were giraffe, zebra, eland, hartebeest, buffalo, and springbok by the hundred. On the first day Stanley shot a springbok and a zebra. He was hot and tired with excitement and the long day's march, and as they were camped in a creek by a deep and cool river he decided to have a swim. He undressed on a grassy slope under the shade of a large mimosa and stood on the edge of the stream with the water lapping over his feet, looking at the lotus leaves and the reflexions. He raised his arms, put his hands together, and leant forward preparatory to diving, but just in time realized he was staring into the jaws of an enormous crocodile.

When he was in a good mood and things had gone well, when there had been plenty of food and the men were cheerful and not tired, they sat together round the fire in the evening and watched the sun setting and the night coming on.

"—this was the time, after our day's work was ended, when we all would produce our pipes, and could best enjoy the labors which we had performed, and the contentment which follows a work well done.

"Outside nothing is heard beyond . . . the hoarse croaking of frogs in the pool hard by, or the song of the crickets . . .; inside our camp are heard the gurgles of the gourd pipes as the men inhale the blue ether which I also love. I am contented and happy, stretched on my carpet under the dome of living foliage, smoking my short meerschaum, indulging in thoughts."

Later he would go into his tent, which was like a bathing-hut, tall and square, with a pointed roof, over which flew the Stars and Stripes. He would light a candle and write his diary, or read the Bible, or look at old copies of the *Herald* and laugh at the remote and unimportant goings-on in the civilized world. At Grant's second presidential levee Mrs. X had worn an overskirt with ruchings of crimson satin; a lavender ostrich plume had waved among the lovely grey curls of Mrs. Y; and Mrs. Z had radiated a blaze of light from her diamonds as she moved along in royal-purple satin.

The most serious trouble he had was another mutiny. The hunting was so good and the men were enjoying it so much, and having such quantities to eat, that although they had been given a halt of three days in which to stock up and rest they begged for one more, and were in a surly temper when he refused it. At dawn on the 7th of October he ordered them to march, but after going for half an hour they threw down their loads. He was walking last, at the end of the caravan, driving the stragglers, and as soon as he caught up and saw what was happening he took his double-barrelled shotgun from Selim, loaded it, and loosened the flaps of his revolver holsters. The men were standing about in groups, and they seized their guns as he appeared. When he got within thirty yards he noticed two men with guns hiding behind an anthill on his left. Aiming from the hip, he ordered them to come out, and they got up and walked slowly towards him, pointing their guns, but one of them sidled off to get behind his back. Stanley allowed this man to get within a few feet and then spun round and knocked him over. He then faced the other—a gigantic man called Asmani, one of the guides—and warned him that if he did not lower his gun instantly his brains would be blown out. Instead, the guide began to raise his gun, but at that moment an old soldier who had served with Speke's expedition several years before ran up from behind and snatched it from him. The guide lost his nerve and fell on his face and begged Stanley's forgiveness.

If Stanley had shown the least hesitation on this occasion he would have lost control of the men and never regained the absolute authority which he was going to need to force them forward through another wilderness and more hostile tribes before reaching Ujiji. But he did not react to danger in that way, and, as always, the least opposition made him so furious and obstinate that he would die rather than change his mind or let a man get away with disobeying an order. He forgave the two men, but he beat and chained the sergeant-major and another senior N.C.O., either of whom could have quelled the rising at the beginning if they had taken a lead and done their duty.

Up to now, on the first arm of the detour, they had been travelling south-west on a recognized route and the going had been fairly easy. But on the 9th of October, because of rumours of a local war ahead of them and also because they were well south of Mirambo, Stanley decided he could safely swing round, and they turned north-west into a more uninhabited jungle, relying on compass and a doubtful map [66] and using elephant tracks and local paths.

Now they began to meet lions and leopards, elephants and rhinoceros; pelicans, storks, cranes, snowy spoonbills, and flamingoes. Food and water were scarce at times. On one day, the 29th of October, they marched without a meal for twenty hours, and all each man had for supper at the end of it was a quart of hot tea with plenty of sugar; that night Stanley carved the date on the trunk of a sycamore and under it "Starving: H. M. S." But this was the last of short rations, and the next morning they reached a wide and populous valley and were able to buy all they wanted. They were now clear of any danger from Mirambo, and had twice had news of Livingstone: once on the 12th of October—rather vaguely, from a caravan, but any report of a white man was encouraging—and the second time now, in the valley, definite news from a party that had actually come from Ujiji only eight days before. A white man had just arrived there, they said, coming from Manyuema, old, dressed like Stanley, with a white beard. He had been there before. He was ill.

Stanley felt absolutely certain that this was the Doctor, and he could hardly contain his excitement. He decided to march on immediately and to do his utmost to outdistance any news of his coming, remembering the opinion of Dr. Kirk at Zanzibar that if Livingstone thought there was another white man in the vicinity he would immediately disappear. He promised everyone an extra eight yards of cloth if they would march to Ujiji without a halt, and they all agreed.

But there arose another imperative reason for getting out of the district quickly. Although the people were friendly and willing to trade, their chiefs made exorbitant demands of tribute. After paying three different chiefs, each of whom swore he was the last, and hearing that the route still lay through the territory of others, relatives of those he had just paid, Stanley determined to escape by a night march. The men muzzled the goats and under a bright moon successfully stole away. This was the 7th of November, and on the night of the 9th they camped at the foot of the hills from the top of which in the morning they would see Ujiji and Lake Tanganyika. Stanley ordered Selim to lay out a new flannel suit, to wax his Wellington boots, chalk his helmet, and fold a new pugaree around it. "Good-night," he wrote in his journal. "Only let one day come again, and we shall see what we shall see."

The next day they got up as usual at sunrise and setting off in tremendous spirits made for the crest of the hill. At the top, after about two hours' marching, they caught the first glimpse of the water dancing and sparkling through the trees in the morning sunlight. They hurried on, determined to get to Ujiji before any of the inhabitants reported their approach. Everyone was dressed in clean white cloths, by Stanley's special order. They were all jubilant, laughing and singing, while Stanley, too, was bursting with excitement. At noon, coming to the top of a ridge, they saw, suddenly, the full expanse of the lake only five hundred yards below them, and at its edge the huts of the village quivering in the hot sun.

They stopped, unfurled their flags, and loaded their guns, and at a one-two-three from Stanley, fired them all simultaneously into the air. This was the recognized signal for the arrival of a caravan outside a village. Then they started marching again, reloading as quickly as they could, and firing as they went.

In a few minutes Ujiji was alive with natives running towards them, and they were soon surrounded by a vast mob of excited men, women, and children, shouting and yelling and pointing at Stanley and the American flag. Above the din Stanley heard someone call "Good morning, sir," and, looking round, he saw a well-dressed, smiling native in a long white shirt and a turban of American sheeting coming towards him.

"Who the mischief are you?"

"I am Susi, the servant of Dr. Livingstone."

"What! Is Dr. Livingstone here?"

"Yes, sir."

"In this village?"

"Yes, sir."

"Are you sure?"

"Sure, sure, sir. Why, I leave him just now."

UJIJI. THE MANGO TREE UNDER WHICH STANLEY
MET LIVINGSTONE IN 1871

Another servant of Livingstone's appeared and introduced himself, one whose name Stanley recognized, and he asked him more questions: how the Doctor was, where had he come from, when had he got back? He asked Susi to run to the Doctor and tell him he was coming, but he forgot to say who he was and Susi forgot to ask him.

By this time they were so close to the village, and the crowd was so thick, that they could hardly move. Suddenly Selim shouted that he could actually see Livingstone, and pointed him out, looking old and pale, with a grey beard, standing in the middle of the village, surrounded by a group of Arabs. Stanley saw him, too, and called the caravan to a halt and stood for a moment looking at him while the crowd became silent and separated, making a lane between them.

Stanley was so excited that he hardly knew what he was doing. He wanted to jump in the air, turn a somersault, and rush up to Livingstone and embrace him. But he stood still, controlling himself, looking towards the Doctor, down the lane of mute faces, reminding himself of the need, even at this time, of keeping up appearances, if only for the sake of discipline, and remembering, too, that the Doctor might not even want to see him.

The Doctor now stood a little way off from the Arabs, alone. He was wearing his Consul's cap—a kind of blue yachting cap with a wide faded gold band on a scarlet ground,[67] a red woollen cardigan,[68] grey tweed trousers, and patent-leather shoes.[69]

Stanley started to walk towards him, coming up from the back of his caravan through the divided ranks of his men, the crowd hushed to absolute silence, watching him. He was preceded by the gigantic guide, Asmani, who had threatened him in the mutiny and who now held aloft the Stars and Stripes on the end of a spear. The guide walked slowly, and Stanley kept equal pace behind him, moving with dignity and deliberation. When he came up to the Doctor he spoke quietly and seriously, took off his hat, bowed, and held out his hand.

"Dr. Livingstone, I presume?"

"Yes," answered the Doctor.

Livingstone bowed and raised his hat too. He looked at Stanley intently, and after a few seconds his face softened and he smiled.

They shook hands, and the Doctor presented Stanley to the Arabs, the principal ones coming forward and being introduced by name, to each of whom Stanley bowed and raised his topee.

Dr. Livingstone then suggested that they go back to his hut because the sun was so hot, and they all turned and went back there and sat down on the long, solid mud bench which was built against the wall under the overhanging eaves. They were followed by the whole crowd of astonished inhabitants. "Both Arabs and natives were delighted at the arrival of the white stranger," says an old account. "They hoisted their flags and beat their tom-toms."

It was just after twelve o'clock on Friday the 3rd of November, 1871,[70] the two hundred and thirty-sixth day of Stanley's march from the coast, the end of a journey of nine hundred and seventy-five miles.[71]

Livingstone was fifty-eight, sick, weary, exhausted by his travels, and soon to die. But Stanley was only thirty, ambitious and tough, destined to follow in the old explorer's footsteps and to consummate his life's work.

Stanley sat on the bench, staring at the great circle of black faces round him, turning occasionally to Livingstone on the one side or to the Arabs on the other, and answering questions. But his mind wandered. The wind rustled the palm branches, and the surf washed up and down on the beach behind him. He felt a little weak and very hungry. He was thirsty, too, and longed for a cup of tea.

Chapter Ten

LIVINGSTONE had reached Ujiji thirteen days before
Stanley arrived, having been away for two years and three
months.[72] All but three of his men had deserted him or refused to go any farther, he had no cloth, and had been without
medicine of any kind for almost five years; he had suffered
terribly from ulcers on his feet which refused to heal, and also
from fever and dysentery. In spite of this he had managed to
reach the great river Lualaba, three hundred miles to the west,
which he knew to be either the Congo or the Nile, and which
Stanley, later, was to trace to the sea and prove to be the
former. But he had been unable to get a canoe to cross it, and
had been forced to turn back and accept the protection of Arab
slavers whose trade he had made it his life's ambition to destroy.
He had returned to Ujiji on the point of collapse, hoping to
find the supplies for which he had written to Kirk in 1869, and
had found only that the whole consignment had been stolen by
the half-caste who had been commissioned to bring it up. All he
had was an ultimate reserve of enough cloth to last a month,
which he had left with a friendly Arab. When Stanley arrived
he had only about a week's supply of this in hand. After that
was finished he would have been destitute, and he had planned
to sell his watch, gun, and instruments, always hoping, despite
the fact that the road was closed by Mirambo, that something
would arrive from Zanzibar before the end. He had been
troubled with his eyes, he was emaciated by dysentery, which
had become chronic, and he had been unable to digest anything
for weeks; he had every reason to think he would soon be dead.

The hut to which he and Stanley and the Arabs now walked
was a low, rectangular, thatched building with mud walls and
wide extensions from the eaves which were propped up at intervals by poles. It faced east and looked across the market-

place to the mountains down which Stanley had just come. Behind it was the lake, and the air was filled with the sound of surf breaking against the shore of the bay. Just before Stanley had arrived, Livingstone had been sitting brooding on the veranda, doing nothing and feeling ill and depressed. He had heard rumours of a white man at Tabora, but had thought he must be a replacement sent by the French Government for a Lieutenant Le Saint,[73] who had died recently near Gondokoro on the Nile. At any rate, whoever it was, he never dreamt it was anything to do with him.

Suddenly, as he had been sitting gazing towards the mountains, he had heard the guns of Stanley's party, and shortly afterwards his servant, Susi, had come running to tell him that a caravan was arriving led by an Englishman. Livingstone could hardly believe it, and had sent him back to make sure and to ask his name. By this time the Arabs had also heard of the approach of a white man and they had all come to Livingstone's hut; then they walked with him to the centre of the market-place, where they stood in a deputation and waited to receive the visitor.

On seeing Stanley, Livingstone's first impression had been amazement at the luxury of his equipment, at his bath, and the number of pots and pans and kettles, and at a gigantic frying-pan about two feet in diameter which was carried like a gun over the shoulder of a native, a kettle inside it, and a bucket swinging on the end of its long handle to even its balance.

"I thank God, Doctor, I have been permitted to see you," Stanley said after they had shaken hands.

Livingstone answered, "I feel thankful that I am here to welcome you."

When he and Stanley got back to his hut he made Stanley sit in his own place—a goatskin stretched over a mat of palm leaves, with another goatskin nailed to the wall to protect his back from the cold mud, and he himself sat down on Stanley's right. The Arabs took their places on Stanley's left, and the whole population of Ujiji, approximately a thousand natives, stood about and watched them. After a short while the Arabs got up and took their leave, and a large part of the crowd went with them.

Livingstone now noticed that Stanley's men were standing round not knowing where to unload, and he immediately invited Stanley to store his equipment in his quarters and take a room there himself, apologizing for not having thought of it sooner.

Stanley thanked him and accepted, and gave orders to the sergeants about storing the goods and buying rations. He then asked the Doctor if he might ask his cook to get some breakfast, as it was long after mid-day and he was hungry. The Doctor at once called his own cook and told her to help Stanley's and between them to make something good.

Stanley remembered Livingstone's letters, and sent for the man who carried them and made him give them to the Doctor with his own hands. Livingstone's eyes lit up as he took the bag, but after opening it and glancing at one or two, he let it rest on his lap, refusing to read any more and begged Stanley to tell him the news of the world. He had been without letters for so many years, he said, that another hour or two could make no difference.

Stanley began talking, and after a while Kalulu and Selim came in and laid a table with a crimson cloth, bringing Stanley's silver teapot full of the best tea, his silver spoons, and best china cups and saucers; as well as porridge, dampers, and yoghurt, honey and fruit from Livingstone's kitchen, presents of curried chicken, rice, stewed goat, and meat cakes began to arrive from the Arabs. Livingstone said grace: "For what we are going to receive, make us, O Lord, sincerely thankful," and they both sat down and began to eat. Stanley suddenly remembered the champagne and the silver goblets and sent Selim to fetch them, and he and the Doctor drank each other's health. Although Livingstone had eaten nothing for weeks, he now felt ravenously hungry and ate everything that was put before him. He could hardly stop eating, and his black lady cook, who had despaired of ever getting him to take anything, kept coming out of the cookhouse to peer at him, quite unable to understand it. He kept on eating and eating, urging Stanley to continue talking, and murmuring over and over, "You have brought me new life; you have brought me new life." During the day they had three large meals and Livingstone went right through all of them without giving it a thought.

Stanley himself was so happy that he hardly knew what was going on. He had thought and dreamed about this meeting for so long that now it was actually taking place he could scarcely believe it. He had meant to take down in shorthand everything that the Doctor said, but he completely forgot. He simply sat, his piercing grey eyes shining with excitement, allowing himself to be prompted into accounts of the news of the world, and drinking in every word that the Doctor uttered.

At last, when it was getting late, the two men got up. The Doctor showed Stanley to his room, in which there was a primitive four-poster [74] with a palm-leaf mattress, and gave him some old copies of *Punch* and the *Saturday Review*.

Stanley thanked him and insisted that he now go and read his letters—he would not keep him up any longer.

"Yes," Livingstone answered, "it is getting late; and I will go and read my friends' letters. Good night, and God bless you."

It was not until the next day that Stanley told the Doctor why he had come and what he was doing, meeting him on the veranda before breakfast. Livingstone said he had, of course, wondered about it, but he had not liked to ask, as he had felt it was none of his business. Stanley opened the conversation by giving him his visiting-card [75] and asking him if he had ever heard of the *New York Herald*, to which the Doctor inappropriately replied, "Oh, who has not heard of that despicable newspaper?" Stanley then explained the object of his expedition, and asked Livingstone if he would mind giving him a letter to Bennett to prove he had seen him. Livingstone readily promised to do so.

Having reached the Doctor, Stanley's main concern now was to get back to report it, so when Livingstone asked him a few days later if he would like to return west to Manyuema with him, he had to refuse. Apart from anything else, the novelty of Africa was beginning to wear off for Stanley and he was sick of struggling with the climate and exhausting himself trying to get some work out of the natives. He suggested instead that they make a short trip to the northern end of the lake to find out if the River Rusizi at its head flowed in or out—a question which was worrying the geographers at home. From something Livingstone had once said, it was now thought possible the outlet was at the north and that the Tanganyika itself might be the ultimate source of the Nile. Livingstone agreed, and they decided to start as soon as he was fit.

In the meantime Livingstone rested and took medicine, and rapidly became much stronger; and Stanley installed his bath, got out his Persian carpet, and made himself and the Doctor cheerful and comfortable. They had four good meals a day instead of the meagre two which Livingstone had eaten previously, and Stanley often cooked special things for him with his own hands. He laid out all his clothes, medicines, and equipment in heaps on the floor of his room and presented half of each to the Doctor; in addition, he gave him a brand-new suit of dark grey Norfolk tweeds which he had bought in Bombay. The Doctor put this on at once, and although it was a little tight in places, he was able to let it out and make it fit perfectly. He was enormously pleased at this, and promised Stanley his Consul's cap in return as a souvenir.

Stanley described him as a little over middle height, slightly bent and stoutish, and moving with a rather slow, heavy tread. He had light brown hair, streaked with grey over the temples, and a very grey beard and moustaches. His face was lined and

gaunt and he had lost most of his teeth, but he had bright hazel
eyes with keen sight, a quiet, jolly sense of humour, and a warm
Scottish accent. Stanley was deeply impressed by his gentleness
to the natives, no matter what they did to him, and by his pro-
found sense of religion and belief in the guidance of Providence.
Like Stanley, he had unusual tenacity and powers of endurance
and an exceptional memory.

Food of all kinds was plentiful—fresh eggs, honey, figs, dates,
apples, radishes, butter, cheese, and a large variety of delicious
fish. The weather was perfect, never more than eighty in the
shade. On Sundays the Doctor held a brief service on the
veranda for his followers, reading the Bible and giving a short
explanatory sermon in Kiswahili. In the mornings and evenings he and Stanley walked together by the shores of the lake,
and in the daytime when they were not working they talked
on the veranda and watched the natives in the market. Ujiji was
a busy place at that time, and at the height of its prosperity, a
great mart for slaves, ivory, household wares, food, and ornaments. It was made up of a straggle of beehive native huts and
Arab houses of sun-dried brick, and on market days as many as
two thousand people swarmed about in it, making a fascinating,
lively, noisy scene.

Every day Stanley grew to like and respect Livingstone more,
and this was a time of great happiness for him. Stanley's rough,
boyish manner, his broad American accent, the very fact that
he was an American—all of which things had drawn snubs and
sniggers from Englishmen in the past—went unnoticed. If anything, they became an advantage to him, since if he had been
an Englishman with his own views about the geography of
Africa and the Nile sources he might have been resented, as Dr.
Kirk implied. But as a foreigner, in no way interested in what
Livingstone was doing, except from an entirely human and
general point of view, he was welcomed with open arms, and
Livingstone in his turn quickly grew to feel a warm and
fatherly affection for him. Stanley was doubly grateful for

this, because he had expected Livingstone to be morose and touchy and only wanting to be left alone. When he had walked towards him at the time of meeting he had braced himself for a tingling snub. He had not forgotten his humiliations in Abyssinia, to say nothing of the behaviour of Dr. Kirk, and Livingstone, as an old associate of Kirk's, might have been expected to deal with him in the same way. But Livingstone treated him as an equal, and Stanley conceived a love and admiration for him that he never lost.

Reflecting about this in his diary on the 16th of November he wrote:

"His manner suits my nature better than that of any man I can remember of late years. Perhaps I should best describe it as benevolently paternal. It is almost tender, though I don't know much about tenderness, but it steals an influence on me without any effort on his part. He does not soften his voice, draw back his lips in an affected smile, mince his words or curtsey to my wish or will, but is sincerely natural, and converses with me as if I were his own age or of equal experience. I get as proud as I can be, as though I had some great honor thrust on me."

The nearest Stanley ever got to a rebuff was one day when he interrupted Livingstone as he was sitting, as he often did, musing and staring into space, frowning and moving his lips and smiling.

"A penny for your thoughts, Doctor," he said.

"They are not worth it, my young friend, and let me suggest that if I had any, possibly I should wish to keep them!"

After this, Stanley held his tongue.

At the end of a fortnight the Doctor felt strong enough to start on the expedition to the head of the lake. They borrowed a canoe from an Arab, a giant hollowed-out tree rowed by sixteen oarsmen who sat side by side in pairs. One of these was Bombay, who was in command, and another was Stanley's cook. There were also two guides, and Selim and Susi. The Union Jack and the Stars and Stripes flew at the bow and stern respectively, and Stanley and Livingstone sat under an awning in the stern and steered.

They reached the head of the lake at the end of the month, established definitely that the Rusizi ran into and not out of it, and returned without incident on the 12th of December, having gone up the eastern shore and come back by the west. Livingstone had a bout of diarrhœa and a bilious attack, and Stanley had two bouts of fever, the first he had suffered since leaving Tabora, but apart from these they both kept well.

"Argued at night about politics with Livingstone," Stanley wrote in the evening of the 24th of November. "He is strong for Disraeli, and I am as strong for Gladstone, but finding my fever increasing, I desisted, and he fell to and nursed and coddled me."

Otherwise they had no troubles or hindrances except the usual demands for tribute at some places where they stopped for the night. Livingstone did the bargaining, and Stanley enjoyed watching his methods and success. He was impressed especially by Livingstone's fatherly calm in dealing with the natives when they were fierce or drunk. Livingstone baffled them; they could not get round him or frighten him or make him lose his temper, and in the end they always gave in. But Stanley was too young and impetuous for this approach, and it irritated him, although he admired it.

On two occasions there were hostile demonstrations against them. During one of these the natives began throwing rocks, and Stanley suggested putting a shot into them, as he certainly would have done if he had been on his own. But the Doctor, although he said nothing, obviously did not approve, and Stanley held his fire. Bombay and Susi got drunk one night when they were supposed to be guarding the canoe, and five hundred rounds of ammunition, ninety musket balls, a large bag of flour, nine hundred fathoms of sounding line, and the whole of the Doctor's stock of white sugar were stolen.

Another night Susi got drunk again and came into the hut which Stanley and Livingstone were sharing and crawled into Livingstone's bed. For some reason Livingstone thought it was Stanley, and made room for him. He was furious when he woke up from cold early in the morning, propped himself up, and discovered Susi with all the blankets. But even then Livingstone only slapped him vigorously on the back with his bare hand until he woke up. Susi was horrified and ashamed, and doubly so that his guilt and punishment should have been seen by Stanley. The only other mishap was that Stanley, too, lost his line and lead, the line breaking when he was pulling it up shortly after they started. On the whole they took things gently, and the Doctor called the trip a picnic. But they did have one long day when hostile natives on the shores prevented their landing and they were forced to row for eighteen hours at a stretch.

On the 9th of December they camped on one of a group of three islets which had not previously been shown on any map, and as they had an unpronounceable native name, Livingstone re-named them the "New York Herald Islets", and shook hands with Stanley to confirm it. They are still called this to-day.

The lake was surrounded on all sides by high mountains, which in some places ran straight to the water but in others came down farther inland, leaving wide stretches of cultivated land. The shores were thickly populated by natives who fished and farmed, whose children played and chased each other in the water. The water was green and very deep, the mountains thickly wooded, and the land more fertile and beautiful than any Stanley had seen. When they got back, Stanley was lucky enough to find some letters from Webb, written in June, but there were none for the Doctor, and he was very disappointed.

Livingstone now settled down to writing to his friends and family and making up his notes, and he also gave Stanley a dictated account of his travels. He discovered from a Nautical Almanac that he was three weeks out in his dates, and that

Stanley, too, had jumped a week. Livingstone also wrote the first of two long letters to Bennett, thanking him warmly for his help and outlining his past travels and plans for the future.

Despite the fact that Livingstone longed to go home to rest and see his family, he was determined to finish his search for the source of the Nile, which he believed would not now take more than eighteen months. After discussing various plans, he decided to go back with Stanley as far as Tabora, collect his goods which had been left in Stanley's enclosure, and wait for Stanley to get to the coast and send back fifty reliable men. With them he would return to Ujiji and continue west. If he could have engaged some of Stanley's men at once he would have done so and set off right away. He was welcome to do so as far as Stanley was concerned, but the men from Zanzibar had only hired themselves for two years and refused to consider anything that might keep them away longer.

This plan of going back to Zanzibar to recruit men for the Doctor was quite convenient to Stanley, and the only difference it made to him was that it forced him to return to civilization via Bombay. He had hoped to avoid doing this, and to have gone north from Tabora instead, across Lake Victoria and down the Nile to Cairo. This route had been pioneered nine years before by Speke and Grant, and Stanley reckoned it would be quicker and more amusing than going back the way he had come. At Cairo there was a cable office, and his chief ambition now was to despatch the news of his success to Bennett as soon as possible. There was a chance, too, that he might have met another famous explorer, Sir Samuel Baker, who was thought to be near Gondokoro. If he could have done this he would have made his scoop even more valuable than it was already. But as Livingstone wished it, he was more than ready to put the idea aside.

Stanley was delighted and full of pride at the thought of Livingstone travelling under his escort, and he busied himself arranging the stores and equipment and apportioning the loads.

He bought Livingstone a donkey, stocked up with milch-goats and fat sheep, and got the Doctor's cook to grind a sackful of fine flour.

For the route, Stanley suggested that they sail down the lake to a point from which they could march directly east and strike the path that he had taken on his way up. By this method he reckoned they would meet no one, avoid Mirambo, and escape having to pay tribute; to all of this the Doctor agreed. Mirambo was still terrorizing the country, and while they were at Ujiji a party of three hundred went off armed with guns to avenge the death of an Arab's son.

On the 20th of December the winter rainy season began and the temperature dropped to 66° F. Two days later Stanley had another attack of fever, but he was carefully looked after by Livingstone, and was well enough on Christmas morning to get up and give special instructions to his cook Feragji about Christmas dinner. He was determined to make it a success, and he ordered sheep, goat, fish, fresh eggs, milk, local toddy, and beer. But Feragji had fallen in love with Dr. Livingstone's cook, Hailima, although she was married, and he spent so much time being tender to her in the cookhouse that he burnt every course to a cinder. Stanley was furious and would have beaten him if he could, and as the most effective alternative he banished him from the kitchen and reduced him to the rank of an ordinary porter. Dr. Livingstone was annoyed too, and recorded in his diary that they had spent a sorry Christmas.

Before they left, Stanley, who could draw well, made a sketch of Livingstone sitting on the veranda. He showed him bareheaded, in his shirt sleeves, writing on his knee in an enormous Lett's Diary, with some sheets of loose paper and a travelling inkpot beside him, a pen in his right hand and two Arabs watching him in the background. He also made a drawing of their house. Although he had no premonitions about ever coming back to Africa or about Livingstone's death, he realized that this was a special moment in his life, and he did all he could to make a clear and vivid record of it. The house was burnt down a few years afterwards, but Stanley's sketch of it is now in the Livingstone Museum in Scotland, and at Ujiji there is a simple monument on which is written:

> "Under the Mango tree
> Which stood here
> Henry M. Stanley met
> David Livingstone,
> 10 November, 1871."

Stanley's final comment in his journal is simple and moving. On the day before they left he wrote that he had been "indescribably happy".

In many ways it was the last completely happy time in his life.

Chapter Eleven

THE day for leaving Ujiji had been settled for the 27th of December, and by eight o'clock that morning everything was ready. The stores for the journey were packed in two canoes so that the porters could march along the lakeside unloaded; at river mouths they were to be met and ferried across by the boats, and their only responsibility was to drive the pack-donkeys, milch-goats, and sheep. Since Livingstone expected to come back in a few months, he left behind one iron and two wooden boxes filled with cloth, beads, tea, coffee, soap, quinine, shirts and shoes, paper and books, a stand for a sextant, and also one long empty wooden box.

At nine o'clock, watched by the Arabs and the whole population, Stanley and Livingstone pushed off in high spirits in a canoe each, Livingstone taking the lead, each steering and each flying his flag from a bamboo. The Doctor was accompanied by his five servants, and Stanley by Selim, and the canoes, as before, were rowed by natives sitting side by side in pairs. Stanley's canoe was larger and its flagpole much taller than the Doctor's, and when the old man saw the Stars and Stripes flying higher than the Union Jack he smiled and warned Stanley that America would get put in her place at the next stop, as he would make a flag pole from the tallest tree in the forest.

The boats started to race, and rushed through the water until the crews collapsed from laughter and exhaustion, and the land party began to race the boats, making terrific efforts whenever they got out of sight behind the trees or headlands, in the hope of being able to reach the other side first. The crews were Ujiji sailors who would return when Stanley and Livingstone landed, but for the shore party it was the start, at last, of the road home, and they were in a frenzy of excitement.

"We have given the Waha, the slip! ha, ha!
The Wavinza will trouble us no more! oh, oh!
Mionvu can get no more cloth from us! hy, hy!
And Kiala will see us no more—never more! he, he!"

they shouted, and the sailors groaned with laughter and exer-
tion and roared the chorus back to them across the water.

The canoe party rowed for a week, making occasional halts,
until they reached the village in the shelter of a great bay sixty
miles south of Ujiji which had been arranged as a rendezvous.
For the first four nights they had made a joint camp with the
shore party, but then they had had to separate because of cliffs,
and there was no news of the others when they landed. But
Stanley had given them eight days' rations when they started,
and at the last halt together he had given them four days more,
and there was no reason to suppose they would not arrive in
due course. As a rallying signal he tied his flag on the end of a
twenty-foot bamboo and lashed it to the top of the tallest tree
in the village, and he and the Doctor unloaded the canoes and
installed themselves to wait. Food began to run low on the
second day and Stanley went hunting with Kalulu, whom he
had taken on board at the last stop, and shot a zebra and a
goose; the next day the land party arrived and pleased Stanley
by reporting that they had seen his flag from more than fifteen
miles away. The canoes had been sent home, and on the 7th,
although Stanley was feverish, they broke camp and headed
east under a guide with a total party of forty-four.

In a speech in England, as quoted in a contemporary book,
he gives this account of their daily journey.

"When we start from our camp in the morning, and give
the word to march, it is tramp, tramp, tramp in dead silence,
in Indian file, through the forest. Every now and then some
fellow has a happy thought, and immediately breaks into
song, and the great forest rings with the chorus. When the
song is ended we go on in that silent Indian file again till perhaps we sight a village. We do not know what the village is.

made some 20 or 30 miles of Southing, a sore heart made still sorer by the sad scenes of man's inhumanity to man made this march a horrible tramp — The sun aurtical and the sore heart reacting on the physical frame, I was in pain nearly every step of the way and arrived a mere ruckle of bones & just myself destitute — I felt as if dying on my feet and lost spirit — I wrote that I was like the man who went from Jerusalem to Jericho but no good Samaritan would come the ajijian way — When just as my thoughts got to the lowest verge — a caravan was reported and one of my men ran in breathless haste gasping out "an Englishman coming" and back he darted to meet him — The American flag at the head of the caravan told of the strangers nationality. He was Henry M Stanley, travelling correspondent of the "New York Herald" sent by the son of the editor, James Gordon Bennett junior to find out where your servant was if alive and if dead to bring home my bones — With characteristic American generosity I was free to all the good he had wrought at & am as cold and £4000. again — demonstrative as we islanders are reputed to be, but this kindness was overwhelming. Here was the good Samaritan and no mistake. never was I more hard pressed — never was help more welcome — my appetite returned — I ate four meals a day instead of the miserable scanty two daily repasts I gorged on myself and in a week felt getting strong again — I

REPRODUCTION OF EXTRACT FROM LETTER FROM LIVINGSTONE TO SIR THOMAS MACLEAR AND MR. MANN, DESCRIBING STANLEY'S ARRIVAL

Is it hostile, or is it friendly? Those are the first questions we ask each other. And the way to find that out is to break into song. The natives hear the strains. If they are friendly they come out to join us; if they are hostile they shut the doors, and as we file past the wicket and the fences we see the scowling faces behind the palisades.

"Then we get into camp. 'Now, boys,' I say, 'pitch the tent and let us have a cup of tea.' [76] That tea is all our refreshment. It is our beer, our champagne and our wine; and after the tea we lie down on the katanda, take out our pipes and smoke. After a smoke we take out our note books and make a record of everything we have found out on the road. That would probably take an hour or half an hour, and it is hard work." [77]

By Stanley's reckoning it was between three and four hundred miles to Tabora, and he expected to strike his old route in about ten days. At the start he relied on the guide, but within a few miles he began to suspect that they were going off course; he took over himself, working with the Doctor's compass from his own map, and on the 17th, to the astonishment of the men and the humiliation of the guide, they reached the summit of the last of a series of ranges and looked down on the plentiful valley through which they had journeyed on their way up. Directly below them lay a large village of over a hundred huts, and the fields were full of the inhabitants weeding and hoeing.

In his excitement he had got far ahead, and it was late at night before the last man arrived. Game had been hard to find, due to the rainy season, and food had been very short, and many of the men were thin and weak. They had all been drenched many times a day by cold rain and by having to ford deep rivers and tramp through dripping, neck-high grass. Stanley himself had been so ridden by fever that he had often only managed to stagger, dazed by quinine, to the end of the day's march, and had been too weak to hunt in the evenings, as he normally did when food was needed. His feet had been very sore and he had cut large holes in the heels of his shoes in an attempt to ease them, and he had even at times allowed himself to ride for a spell on the Doctor's donkey. Livingstone also had been exhausted by the rough going and his feet were swollen and bleeding, and he, too, had been forced to slit his shoes, although they were already in ribbons.

From now on there was plenty of game, and as soon as he was rested Stanley went out with the Doctor's Reilly—a heavy, accurate, double-barrelled rifle. Near the lake he had used it successfully against a buffalo, and two days after reaching the valley he killed two zebras. His pride in this achievement was damped by the men giving all the praise to the rifle, but the Doctor was delighted, and Bombay was very pleased because he had foreseen it in a dream, Stanley having appeared to him with the famous weapon, shooting animals right and left. A few days later he unluckily missed getting a shot at a lion, but when he had hit several giraffe without killing them, at the Doctor's suggestion he melted his zinc canteens and made bullets out of them, and with the first of these bullets he brought down a giraffe at a hundred and seventy-five yards.

He found the Doctor an ideal travelling companion, full of knowledge for emergencies, always ready to cheer him up when he needed it, to sympathize and encourage, to share in his enthusiasm when he was pleased about something, and to nurse him when he was sick. After reaching the old route he had several prostrating bouts of fever. On the 27th he was in bed, unable to move for three days, and again on the 3rd of February, when Livingstone noted in his diary: "Mr. Stanley has severe fever, with great pains in the back and loins: an emetic helped him a little, but resin of jalap would have cured him quickly." On the 4th: "Mr. Stanley so ill that we carried him in a cot." And on the 5th: "Off at 6 a.m. Mr. Stanley a little better, but still carried across same level forest."

During one of these attacks, when he was half crazy from

having taken huge doses of quinine, he sharply complained to the Doctor's cook of the dirty state of the utensils, showing him a coffee-pot thick with verdigris and telling him that everything tasted of it and that all the pots must be cleaned at once. The cook answered that Livingstone had not complained, and that what was good enough for him should be good enough for Stanley. Stanley knocked him down, and the cook went for him.

At this moment the Doctor came out of his tent to see what was wrong, and Stanley explained, shaking with rage and fever, tears of fury running down his cheeks. The Doctor lectured the cook and told him to apologize, but when the cook did so and wished to kiss Stanley's feet, Stanley refused to let him. Then Livingstone took Stanley by the arm and led him back to the tent, telling him not to be upset, the man was only a half-educated savage, and had meant no harm. Stanley brooded all day, but in the evening he went to the cook and they shook hands.

His own account of these fevers is vivid and frightening.

"Am carried again as I cannot even ride my donkey [he wrote on the 13th of February in his journal]. I am in such a state tonight that I can neither lie down or sit quietly in one position long. Livingstone is calmly asleep—I am nervous and my head is very strange. I have the most fearful dreams every night and am afraid to shut my eyes lest I shall see the horrid things that haunt me. I will go walk, walk, walk in the forest to get rid of them."

"*February the 14th.*

"Last night I travelled round and round the camp among the camp fires, stopping a little at one and then at another and then resuming my midnight walk. It must have been two o'clock in the morning before I lay down. I think it must be the quinine which I have taken in unusual doses that created this extraordinary state of nervousness of the head. After a hard wrestling with myself I fell asleep and woke up relieved."

In between whiles he was quite well, and one day they did a march of eighteen miles. This day they were attacked by a swarm of bees which stung Livingstone terribly on the face and head and killed his donkey. Everyone else took to their heels, but the donkey threw Livingstone and stayed in the same place, rolling over and over, and the old man was forced to shelter in a bush and swat the bees with a branch. But in spite of his sore feet and the pain of the stings he refused to be helped, and marched on. He got left so far behind, however, that eventually Stanley sent back two men with a hammock to carry him. Livingstone was furious at this, and shouted at the men to get away—did they suppose he was only a feeble old woman?

When the men came back and related this retort, Stanley became nervous, for Livingstone could be alarming when he was angry. He determined to do what he could to soothe the Doctor before he himself appeared, and ordered the Doctor's servant to make his bed, put out his slippers, and be ready to pull off his shoes the moment he arrived. In addition to this, Stanley ordered the cook to prepare a specially good supper of tea, baked meat balls, and custard. Then he posted two scouts to report the Doctor's approach, and when they gave the signal he hid behind a tree.

Livingstone came slowly into camp, went to his tent, and sat down on the bed. His servant ran in, pulled off his shoes, washed his feet, and put on his slippers, and then fetched the supper and laid it on the table. Livingstone sat for a while resting, the steam from the dishes curling round his head, and finally he rubbed his face in his hands, went over to the table, and began to eat.

After about ten minutes Stanley decided it was safe to appear, and he strolled up and called out "Good evening", as though nothing had happened.

"The Doctor was very grim at first, but he soon relaxed," Stanley recorded. "A good hot meal is a great restorer of the spirits!"

This ability to eat, even when he was exhausted, was one of Livingstone's great strengths, and no matter how tired he was or how meagre the diet, he was always able to fill himself, even when there was nothing but tea or coffee and dampers. When Stanley was ill he sickened against these things and often could take hardly anything. "Five hundred dollars for a loaf of bread!" he wrote; and in his fever he dreamt gluttonously of feasts of bread and butter, and biscuits and cheese, and caviare and ham and jelly.

Just before his last illness, on the 1st of February, they had met a caravan from Tabora bound for Ujiji. Word had got back that the white man had found a safe route, and several traders had begun to use it. There was good news about Mirambo: that he had tried to sue for peace, that the Arabs had refused his offer, and that he was now starving and on the run. There was the good news also that several boxes and packets of letters and papers had arrived for Stanley from Zanzibar. On the bad side, they learnt that Shaw had died soon after he got back and had been buried under a banyan tree near Stanley's hut; also that many Arabs had been killed by smallpox both at Tabora and on the coast. Stanley himself began to wonder if he would survive, but Livingstone assured him that if he had been going to die he would have done so during his illness at Ujiji before Christmas—he was sick now only because of the wet; Shaw had died because of his vices, and Stanley had warned him that he would.

Except for Shaw's death this first contact with the outside world put them in good spirits, the Doctor tantalized Stanley with details of the luxuries stored at Tabora,[78] and when they camped in a deserted stockade near which there happened to

be a large tree, Stanley carved their initials on the trunk, and
the date—February the 2nd, 1872.

When he had heard that there was mail for him, he had sent
his cook forward to collect it, and a fortnight later, on the 14th,
the cook returned, bringing with him the three men who had
been sent to the coast for special medicine for Shaw the previous
August. They had got back to Tabora safely, but nearly two
months after Stanley had left. At Tabora they had caught one
of his deserters, whom they brought with them now, his neck
yoked in the cleft of a stick.

The mail consisted of seven packets, including one from Dr.
Kirk, in which there were three letters for Livingstone and one
for Stanley. Kirk had discovered what Stanley's real mission
was by this time, and now asked him to take charge of
Livingstone's stores and deliver them if he could. Stanley
laughed at this, and said something about it to Livingstone, but
the old man was deep in his own letters and did not hear him.

There were nearly a hundred papers, and the natives were
absorbed by such a quantity and by their huge size, and mystified by the sight of the two men staring at them without saying
anything. Stanley was much amused by this, and although the
papers themselves depressed him with their accounts of the
destruction and bloodshed in Paris during the insurrection of
the Commune, he was cheered by *Punch*.

Once again, on the 13th, he was down with fever, but after
that he remained well, and five days later they reached the wide
valley in which lay his old encampment. Everything seemed in
order, and with pride and happiness he took Livingstone by
the arm and escorted him in.

"Doctor, we are at last *home*," he said.

Livingstone's reply is not recorded, but in his diary for that
night he thanked God for their safe arrival.

This last journey from Ujiji had taken fifty-three days, Stanley
had been away from Tabora for almost exactly five months and
during that time had travelled more than twelve hundred miles.

Chapter Twelve

AS soon as they were settled, Stanley ordered the Doctor's cases of provisions to be brought and they broke them open with a hammer and chisel. One case of brandy was missing, otherwise everything appeared to be intact; but on examining them closely they found very little, and Stanley could not resist making fun of the remains at Dr. Kirk's expense.

In the first box were three tins of biscuits (only one undamaged), six small tins of potted ham, five one-pound stone jars of jam, and three bottles of curry. In the second box were two large Dutch cheeses, one hollow and the other as hard as a brick. In the third were two lumps of sugar; in the fourth candles; in the fifth essence of anchovies, mustard, pepper, and salt, and bottles of Harvey, Reading, and Worcester sauces; and in five others there was only potted meat and meat soup.

The eleventh box proved better, with four flannel shirts, two pairs of English boots, some stockings and shoe-laces, and Livingstone was so pleased with the boots that he tried them on straight away. But on checking the rest of the stores they found that two bales of cloth and four bags of the most valuable type of red coral beads had disappeared. Stanley also discovered that his bales had been tampered with, and, acting on information, he went to the headman of Livingstone's party and questioned him. He found in his kit three hundred and four yards of coloured cloth stamped with the *Herald* Expedition's mark, and when the man also admitted that he knew about the missing brandy, Livingstone immediately dismissed him.

When he had sorted everything out, Stanley was able to give the Doctor forty loads, which made up a total of seventy and was enough for sixty men for four years. As well as twelve bales of cloth, sixteen sacks of beads, and 350 lb. of brass wire, he gave him a revolver, three rifles, and nearly two thousand rounds for each, a boat with 60 lb. of ship's copper, two barrels of tar, and a bag of carpenter's tools, all his extra medicines, utensils, and books, some jackets and trousers, a tent, an air-bed, and a bath. All that Livingstone now needed was porters, and Stanley agreed to send up fifty free men (the men sent up by the British Consul in the past had been slaves), and arm them with a gun and a hatchet each, and two thousand bullets, a thousand flints and ten kegs of gunpowder. Their contract was to be for two years from the date of their arrival at Tabora, and they were to bring with them the last few things that were outstanding: needles and thread, official envelopes, a blank journal, a Nautical Almanac for 1872 and 1873, a slave-chain, a stop-watch, and some tins of sardines and salmon, preserved fruit, biscuits, American wheat-flour, and 10 lb. of China tea.

Stanley decided that as Christmas dinner had been such a failure they ought to celebrate it again, especially as the Doctor had just received from an Arab two bottles of Hennessy—almost all that was left of a large box of various goods consigned to Ujiji five years before; Stanley himself had found some fine old brandy also and one bottle of champagne. They decided to have the party on the 27th of February, and this time it was a great success. "To-day we hold a Christmas feast," Livingstone recorded in his diary, and Stanley was willing to bet that there had never been such a spread in any native house in Africa.

The Doctor was still busy finishing his journal, which covered the whole six years of his last journey, and when this was done he addressed it to his daughter, Agnes, and gave it to Stanley, sealed in five places with an American gold coin, an anna, a half anna, and a cake of paint stamped with the royal arms. Stanley wrapped it in waterproof canvas and wrote on both sides in Gothic letters "POSITIVELY NOT TO BE OPENED", below which Livingstone put his signature.[79] As well as this, Livingstone gave him one letter for Zanzibar, six for Bombay, twenty for Great Britain, and two for New York (these being for Bennett), and dictated detailed instructions about the delivery of various souvenirs. He also gave him a blank receipt addressed to any captain of the Royal Navy who could be persuaded to part with a chronometer, and a cheque for £500 to pay Kirk for stores if he needed it. All these things were packed in a black tin box. Finally the Arabs, too, gave Stanley forty-five letters for Zanzibar.

It was now settled that Stanley should leave on the 14th of March: the winter rainy season had come to an end, all the stores had been checked and made over, and there was nothing more he could do. His only remaining responsibility was to get to the coast as quickly as possible and send back the porters so that Livingstone could get away. The last thing he and Livingstone did together was to build a huge mound of stones eight feet long and five broad to mark Shaw's grave.[80] It took fifty men two days, and Livingstone predicted that it would stand for hundreds of years and be a permanent memorial to the first white man to die in Tabora.

The night before Stanley left, all the men gathered outside his hut for a farewell dance. Four drummers stood in the centre of a ring, beating with a steady, furious rhythm, and one by one the others stepped out and performed. The cook who had fought Stanley, and Asmani, the gigantic guide who had threatened to shoot him, thrashed the air with their weapons, while the man who had saved him in the mutiny gyrated like an elephant. Bombay paraded with Stanley's water-bucket on his head, and another man veiled himself with a goatskin and whirled an axe. A fifth darted into Stanley's room and snatched a spear, and then, to the intense admiration of the whole company, Stanley himself suddenly jumped to his feet, sprang into the ring, and capered like a madman.

Then the rhythm changed and the men began singing:

Leader: "Oh oh oh! The white man is going home!"
Chorus: "Oh oh oh! Going home, going home! Oh oh oh!"

Leader: "To the happy island on the sea
　　　Where the beads are plenty! Oh oh oh!"
Chorus: "Oh oh oh! Where the beads are plenty! Oh oh oh!
Leader: "While Singiri has kept us, oh, very long
　　　From our homes very long! Oh oh oh!
Chorus: "From our homes, oh oh oh! Oh oh oh!
Leader: "And we have had no food for very long—
　　　We are half-starved, oh, for so long!
　　　　　Bana Singiri!
Chorus: "For so very long, oh oh oh!
　　　Bana Singiri-Singiri!
　　　Singiri, oh, Singiri!
Leader: "Mirambo has gone to war to fight against the Arabs;
　　　The Arabs and the Wangwana have gone to fight Mirambo!
Chorus: "Oh oh oh! To fight Mirambo!
　　　　Oh Mirambo, Mirambo!
　　　　Oh, to fight Mirambo!
Leader: "But the white man will make us glad,
　　　He is going home! For he is going home,
　　　And he will make us glad! Sh sh sh!
Chorus: "The white man will make us glad!
　　　　Sh sh sh!
　　　　Um um um!
　　　　Sh!"

It was a bright starlit night, and Stanley, going back to the veranda of the house and sitting down beside Livingstone, was excited and moved. When it was all over they went indoors to talk for a short while before going to bed. They both felt the coming separation keenly, and this night Stanley took down in shorthand every word that the Doctor said and guarded the record jealously and never allowed it to be printed. The Doctor half-heartedly tried to persuade him to wait for another month, until the end of the spring rainy season, which would begin shortly, but neither of them really wanted to delay, and Stanley refused to consider it. He had travelled through two rainy seasons, and one more was not worth worrying about. They went to bed late, and he determined to start as arranged at dawn.

In fact they did get up as soon as it was light, and the baggage was brought out of the hut and stacked ready. But they lingered over breakfast without either of them being able to eat anything, and it was past eight o'clock before Stanley finally gave the order to march. Just before they left, the Doctor gave him one last instruction: a note authorizing him to turn back any caravan intended for himself if it was manned by slaves and not freemen. Livingstone had suffered great inconvenience by being sent untrustworthy men in the last few years, and he was determined not to have any more of them.

Then Stanley's men picked up their loads and defiled out of the enclosure shouting a song, and Stanley walked after them. The Doctor stayed at his side, and when they started to climb the low hills on the far side of the valley, and it was time for him to leave, Stanley could hardly keep back his tears. They stopped a little way up, and he turned and looked back for a long time at his old house, now quite small in the distance, and then at the Doctor's lined and bearded face, which had suddenly paled.

"Now, my dear Doctor, the best of friends must part. You have come far enough and the sun is very hot; let me beg of you to turn back."

"Well, I will say this to you: you have done what few men could do—far better than some great travellers I know. And I am grateful to you for what you have done for me. God guide you safe home, and bless you, my friend."

They shook hands, and Stanley tried to hurry on before he broke down, but Susi and two other servants ran forward to shake and kiss his hands, and he was no longer able to control himself, and the tears ran down his cheeks. When all the farewells were over at last he turned quickly towards the caravan, which had come to a halt a little way ahead, and shouted angrily at them to get a move on and not to waste time hanging about watching trifles. The Doctor stood looking after them until all but Stanley had disappeared over the brow of the hill, and when he too reached it he turned and waved his handkerchief, and the old man waved back with his peaked cap. It was

about eleven o'clock on Thursday the 14th of March, 1872, and
no white man was ever to see Livingstone alive again.

"May the Almighty help me to finish my work this year for
Christ's sake!" had been the first entry of the year in the old
man's diary. But he was to die of dysentery seventeen months
later in a native village five hundred miles south of Ujiji, still
searching for the source of the Nile, but hopelessly off the
track. The "great river" which he was tracing was the Congo,
and the Nile rose in Lake Victoria, almost a thousand miles to
the north.

Chapter Thirteen

STANLEY had left two men behind at Tabora who were to stay for two days, in case of last messages, and then catch him up. On the 20th they arrived, accompanied by Susi and another man, and they brought a few more letters from the Arabs and two from Livingstone, one for the Cape of Good Hope, and one for Stanley himself, addressed to "Henry M. Stanley, Esq. Wherever he may be found." Livingstone had no further news, and had been busy copying out some observations which he had made on a journey some years before.

Stanley's answer to this letter has luckily survived, and it shows, as nothing else could, how fond he had become of the Doctor and how genuine was his distress at leaving him. Stanley repeatedly spoke of this parting afterwards,[81] and his unhappiness was so sharp that he never forgot a single detail of it for the rest of his life, and long after his death the 14th of March was remembered in his family as a special day.[82] Particularly since he had expected Livingstone to snub him, the old man's friendliness and admiration had quickly made him feel as he had felt only once before to any other person—the travelling salesman, his foster-father—and Livingstone, for his part, returned the friendship and spoke of Stanley as having behaved towards him with a sense of duty worthy of a son.[83]

Stanley's letter, dated 20th of March, 1872, begins with several paragraphs on various topics, that he had suffered a touch of fever, that his men were marching well, and then continues:

"My dear Doctor, very few amongst men have I found I so much got to love as yourself. In the qualities which go to make the man and the gentleman I find you possess more than any other that I remember. As such should I like to renew our acquaintance if it please God to spare us both until you have finished your labours in the cause of geography, and of course I should like to see once more the Traveller whom I met in Central Africa. I am happy in doing you a service, for then I feel I am not quite separated from you. I wish it were a series of services for then I would feel as if I were with you all the time. I felt very much depressed the whole day, melancholy and lonely. Were it not that I feel a sort of prescience that I shall see you again I should be tempted to return and take one more look and pass a few more hours now. But God's will be done, and England and America expect their people to do their duty. Do you yours as persistently as heretofore and come back to your friends and country to be crowned with the laurel, and I will go forth and do mine, and may God watch over and bless us both shall be my prayer.[84]

"Devotedly yours,
Henry M. Stanley."

Up to this point Stanley had not pressed forward more quickly than normal, to ensure that his two men would over-take him, but from now on he drove the caravan with ferocious energy in spite of the heavy rain of the spring rainy season, which had started three days after they left. In his confidence and impatience he refused to waste time haggling over tribute, as he had on his way up, and one day, when the emissary of a chief started bargaining, he seized him by the throat and threatened to break his nose if he did not accept what was offered at once. Even in the land of the fierce Wagogo they experienced only one incident, when, having passed a village and halted a little way on the far side to get out the tribute, they were suddenly sprung upon by fifty excited savages with strung arrows and ready spears, who demanded threateningly why the traveller had dared to pass them without paying any-thing. Stanley, who was sitting on a bale, kept his head and did not even get up, but firmly asked them what the matter was and pointed to Bombay, who was in the act of breaking open a bale and getting out some cloth. The leader was taken aback and began to laugh, and then, feeling ashamed, accepted a much smaller payment than he might otherwise have done.

For the next five days they marched on in pelting rain and in the face of a piercing wind that howled off the distant mountains ahead, until on the 7th of April they reached Mpwapwa, three hundred and thirty-eight miles from Tabora, having made an average of fourteen miles a day.

It was here that Farquhar had died, and Stanley heard the details from the chief to whose care he had been entrusted, and was shown the spot under a large tree where his body had been covered with leaves and left. Although they searched carefully, they could not find his bones, but in his memory they built a mound of rocks in a hollow at the side of a stream.[85]

On the 12th they reached one of the main rivers which ran down to the thirty-mile-wide valley-swamp of the Makata. From their experience of the year before, and from the tremendous volume of water, they realized that this was an exceptionally wet season, and they followed along the river-bank with every possible energy, in the hope of being able to reach and cross the valley before it became impassable. They were already alternately up to the neck in water and up to the armpits in mud, and so ferociously attacked at night by black mosquitoes that even though they were exhausted they could hardly sleep.

Livingstone's black tin box, containing all his papers and his journal, was nearly lost in a deep, fast river which the men had bridged by felling a tree. The men were climbing across it, Stanley having gone first, when one of them who had not yet crossed suddenly swung the box on to his head and plunged into the middle of the river, falling into a deep hole up to his neck. "Look out! Drop that box and I'll shoot you," Stanley roared at him, drawing his revolver and taking aim. The men on the bridge were tense with excitement, and the man with the box groaned with fright. But he reached the other side safely, and Stanley was so relieved that he only punished him by ordering him never to touch the box again.

About an hour after this they had to cross the main river along which they had been marching. It was in full flood, and after making a raft which quickly sank, they joined all their rope, and a man swam across with it and tied it to a tree. They then pulled themselves over one by one, dragging their loads. This did no harm to the cloth, but it was out of the question for the boxes of papers, and for the rest of that day Stanley could think of no way of transporting them. Finally they camped in two parties, one on either side of the river, hoping that the water might fall by the morning, and in imminent danger that it might rise and sweep them away. The next day the river was as high as ever, and they were no better off, until Stanley was struck by the idea of making stretchers on to which the cases could be lashed and carried on the shoulders of two men. These were quickly made, the strongest swimmers were each given a glass of brandy, and in a short while all the boxes were safely across.

In spite of their hopes and the speed at which they had travelled, when they reached the valley it was too flooded to attempt to cross it, and they had to camp on a small hill for ten days until the rain stopped. Then they plunged in, the water still up to their necks, and for two days waded and swam, tormented by mosquitoes, to the far side, along which ran the actual river itself. They began to cross this at 5 a.m. on the 27th, swimming and wading, every man now carrying only cloth which was his own, as Stanley had given it all out as encouragement. One more river was beyond this one; once across that they climbed up to dry, hard ground and strode forward, thankful and exhausted, for two more days until they reached Simbamwenni.

As before, the bugs here were frightful: scorpions and ants that stung the men's legs as they marched, boas hanging from my dear doctor, very few amongst men have I found I so much got to love as yourself, for the qualities which go to make the man & the gentleman I find you possess more than any other that I remember. As such should I like to renew our acquaintance if it please God to spare us both until

with you all the time. I felt very much depressed the whole day — melancholy & lonely. There is not that I feel a sort of prescience that I shall see you again. I should be tempted to return & take one more look & pass a few more hours now. But God's will be done, and England and America expect their people to do their duty. Do you yours as persistently as heretofore & come back to your friends & country, to be crowned with the laurel, and I will go forth & do mine. And may God watch over & bless us both. Shall be my prayer.

Devotedly yours,

Henry M Stanley

REPRODUCTION OF EXTRACT FROM LETTER
TO LIVINGSTONE FROM STANLEY

the trees, land crabs and iguanas and terrapins. There was further evidence of the exceptional ferocity of the rain. A wall of water had suddenly rushed down the river by the city in the middle of the night and swept away the whole fortified front wall and dozens of houses and inhabitants. Huge trees had been laid flat in swathes, and there were fearful accounts of a tornado that had struck the coast.

Three weeks earlier Stanley had sent ahead three men with despatches for the *New York Herald* and a letter to the American Consul at Zanzibar asking for some luxuries. These men got back on the 2nd of May with some champagne, jam, and biscuits, and some recent copies of the *New York Herald*, in one of which was Stanley's first despatch, written from Tabora the year before. There were also copies of other American papers, and for the first time Stanley learnt with astonishment that his expedition had been the cause of widespread disbelief and amusement. But he was so certain of getting home now, and had such cast-iron proofs of his success, that he was able to laugh it off. For the first time, too, he learnt of the presence of white men at Bagamoyo, on the coast, in command of a "Livingstone Search and Relief Expedition", but he had no idea what this was or who they could be.

Four days later, on the 6th of May, they reached Bagamoyo at sunset. The tattered remains of the Stars and Stripes were hoisted on the boar-spear, the men fired every last grain of powder, and all the inhabitants came out to meet them.

The year before they had taken three months to do this last stage of five hundred and twenty-five miles; now they had done it in thirty-five days. It was their four hundred and eleventh day since leaving, and altogether they had done two thousand two hundred and fifty miles. Eighteen porters and soldiers had died, as well as both the white men, and Stanley himself had had one attack of acute dysentery and twenty-three of severe fever. He had lost 76 lb. and now weighed only seven stone, his thick black hair had become streaked with grey and his round, boyish face had become gaunt and boney. But none of these things mattered in the least, and at that moment he had not even computed them.

To have found Livingstone and saved his life, and explored with him and shared his friendship, had been the most triumphant and dramatic experience of his life, and a far greater reward than anything he had ever dreamed of. He had seen in the old man his ideal of a Christian, a man of almost superhuman capacity, inflexible in what he considered to be his duty, yet completely humble and gentle. He had felt towards him as a disciple and a son, and he knew that his example would be a strength and guidance to him for the rest of his life.

But he had also achieved something that most people considered impossible, and was safely back and could prove it. As a newspaper-man, to have interviewed such a mythical traveller in the middle of the African jungle was a scoop that would electrify his colleagues and astonish the world, and at one stroke establish him as the toughest and most exceptional correspondent of his time. In a few weeks the meeting would be known beyond the farthest reaches of the telegraph, he would be famous and rich, and his name would be a household word, linked for ever with that of the great explorer.

When he thought of all this he regretted nothing, and walked happily down the one street in the twilight between the palms and the thatched mud houses, deafened by the hubbub of the inhabitants, until he came to the middle of the town. There a young man with reddish whiskers, in a topee and flannels, came out of a large white house and walked over to him.

"Splendid success!" exclaimed the young man.

Stanley, without shyness or reserve, thanked him and grinned triumphantly. He almost hugged him in his excitement.

Then they both went indoors and had some beer.

PART TWO

The Disaster

"Charge, Bennett, Charge! On, Stanley, on!
So came last news from Livingstone."
                    Punch, 3rd August 1872.
            (With apologies to Sir Walter Scott.)

Chapter Fourteen

MANY things of extraordinary interest had happened in the world since Stanley had been away from it. Within the first two years of his wanderings every triumph and disaster known to civilization had taken place. There had been the Franco-Prussian War, the rise of the German Empire under the leadership of Prussia, the seizure of Rome from the Pope by the King of the Italians, the denunciation of the Crimean peace treaty by the Russians, and the terrible and bloody revolution of the Commune in Paris.

There had been the wreck of the Royal Navy's finest man-of-war, the "Captain", which had gone down with all five hundred hands in the Bay of Biscay; the great fire of Chicago, which had consumed the homes of more than one hundred thousand people; the proclamation by the Pope of the new dogma of Infallibility, and the famous escape in a balloon from the siege of Paris by Gambetta.

In England the first full-scale manœuvres in the history of the British army had taken place on Chobham Common. Every retired military man in the kingdom had followed them in the papers with the keenest delight, and every one of them had reached the same pleasing conclusion: that all the commanders had bungled everything disgracefully. In addition to this, the attention of the entire population had been transfixed by a court action known as the Tichborne case, a trial of extraordinary complexity in which an Australian butcher called Tom Castro, alias Arthur Orton, claimed to be a long-lost Hampshire baronet.

Finally, some great men had died: Alexander Dumas and Charles Dickens; the great Lord Derby and the veteran Secretary of State, Lord Clarendon, whose position at the Foreign Office had been taken by Lord Granville. Death had also claimed Sir Roderick Murchison, the well-known president of the Royal Geographical Society, at whose request Dr. Livingstone had gone again into the jungle in 1866. In the spring of 1871 the presidency had been filled by the distinguished public servant and archæologist, Major-General Sir Henry Creswicke Rawlinson.

There had been no news of Dr. Livingstone during this time, and not a single word had been received from him since his last letter of May 1869, a period now of almost two and a half years. On the whole, however, no one had worried about him, although a small but increasing number of people were beginning to think he must be dead.

There had also been no accurate news of Stanley, and only two misleading rumours. The first had been on the 19th of September 1871, when the *New York Herald* had published a hint about his expedition but withheld his name. Under the headline "DR. LIVINGSTONE" there had been the following communiqué:

"Advices from Zanzibar announce the receipt of positive intelligence of the safety of Dr. Livingstone. The authority for the statement is unquestionable and its truth certain. A party of Americans is hurrying into the interior with the object of rescuing the doctor from his perilous position."

No one had paid the slightest attention to this announcement, but that was not surprising, since the *Herald* was notorious for publishing any fairy story that came into Bennett's head.

The second report had been two months later, when word had reached London of Stanley's arrival in Zanzibar and the rather mysterious circumstances of his departure with an enormous expedition. Dr. Kirk, the British consul, had written to the president of the Geographical Society about him, describing him as "a man of the true exploring type".[1] But although Dr. Kirk had found out that Stanley was the newspaper correspondent who had achieved the famous scoop at the end of the Abyssinian campaign,[2] he had failed to attach any importance to this fact. He had not mentioned it in his letter, and had not discovered that the *Herald* was financing the present expedition. He had believed that Stanley was going off at his own expense for fun, and that his idea of visiting Dr. Livingstone was nothing more than a social call before he pushed on somewhere else. The president of the Geographical Society had passed on these conclusions to the members, and a résumé of them had appeared in the papers.[3] He had added that he wished Stanley luck, and promised him a great welcome if he returned with authentic news or, better still, brought Livingstone back to civilization.

These rumours and reports constituted the sum total of all that had appeared in the outside world about Stanley and Livingstone between the autumn of 1869 and their meeting twenty-five months later, in November 1871. Of Stanley there had been two inaccurate statements, and of Livingstone there had been nothing—not a single report, note, or message of any kind. But so far as the latter was concerned, this state of affairs had been allowed to go on because no one had worried about him, and the public had believed the Geographical Society were right when they had announced from time to time that he was probably safe.

Suddenly, however, at the end of November 1871, there came a change, and it is at this point that, so far as England is concerned, the history of Stanley and Livingstone really begins. At this point, too, a third character became involved in the drama—Sir Henry Rawlinson, the new president of the Geographical Society, the man who had promised Stanley a hearty welcome if he returned with news of Livingstone. And this promise unknown to Sir Henry, was the first of many ironies to come.

Sir Henry Rawlinson was famous for having deciphered

the great cuneiform inscription at Behistun in Persia, and
for being one of the first men to solve the mystery of the
cuneiform alphabet. But he was also well known as a soldier
and administrator. Born in 1810, he had started his career
as a cadet under the East India Company, had fought with
distinction in the Afghan war, had served as political agent
in Baghdad and as British ambassador in Persia, and had
retired with a knighthood and the rank of major-general. He
had been a member of Parliament twice, was a crown director
of the East India Company, a trustee of the British Museum,
and a member of the India Council—the small committee of
experts who advised the Secretary of State for India. He had
also written several books and had a wide reputation for
classical scholarship. In character he was genial but firm, a large
man with a decisive face, an enthusiastic sportsman, and a good
story-teller, and he was much loved by all who knew him well.
But shy people found him abrupt, and he was impatient with
fools and people who were tiresome. He had made a success of
his life, his opinion was usually accepted as being valuable, and
he was not in the habit of having little men get the better of
him.

On the 27th of November, 1871, the day on which the first
event in this story took place, Sir Henry received a further
letter from Dr. Kirk about Stanley and his progress to Ujiji. So
far as Sir Henry was concerned, it was bad news, for it brought
the first report of the Arab defeat at Tabora by Mirambo and of
Stanley's part in it, with the loss, according to Dr. Kirk, of most
of his men and stores. This meant that there could be small
hope of Stanley's going much farther and, consequently, of his
reaching Livingstone and getting word of him. Sir Henry was
disappointed at this, and as there happened to be a meeting of
the Society on that day, he passed on the information to the
members at once and raised the point as to whether this up-
rising would have any effect on the safety of Dr. Livingstone.
Since Captain Richard Burton, the first European ever to visit

Tabora and Ujiji, was present, Sir Henry asked for an opinion from him.

Captain Burton said without hesitation that Mirambo's war would make no difference to the Doctor. These tribal disturbances were always breaking out in Africa, and they often lasted for several years, but to a man of Livingstone's experience they presented no hazard whatsoever. He would be bound to hear of it, and if he wanted to return to Zanzibar, he could easily avoid Tabora by making a detour to the south. The members could be quite certain that he was all right, because if anything had happened to him they would have heard of it already. Any report of his death would be spread by the natives across the whole continent almost with the speed of the telegraph. Captain Burton himself felt not the slightest anxiety over him, and he was fully convinced that the explorer was safe.

This disposed of the question of Livingstone's safety satisfactorily as far as the Society were concerned, and before they went on to the business of the day—a lecture on the volcanic region east of Damascus—it only remained for them to reflect for a moment on the fate of the young American, Mr. Stanley, besieged at Tabora by howling savages. Sir Henry had just one thing to say about him. Some of the newspapers[4] had published a statement, which had caused immense joy to all explorers, to the effect that after the fight with Mirambo, Stanley had taken to his bed in a serious condition, "ill of fear". Sir Henry Rawlinson, who loved a good joke and was an expert raconteur, now gave himself the exquisite pleasure of referring to this incident. He was happy to say that the whole thing had been a mistake. The young man had not been ill with fear. Furthermore, he had not, as some members had suggested, died of fright. No, no. There had been a misprint which it was now his happy duty to correct. The offending sentence should not have read "ill of fear". but "ill of *fever*"!

There was an uproar of laughter at this, and it was some

minutes before the members became quiet again. Then they forgot about Stanley and settled down to listen to the paper on volcanoes.

But for Stanley, who was at this time floating happily on Lake Tanganyika with Dr. Livingstone, it was a fatal moment. The misprint gave rise to the popular impression that there was something ridiculous about him, and although it was corrected, it led to the first of the jokes at his expense which dogged him for the rest of his life. The laughter had begun.

This meeting of the Geographical Society provoked one of those eruptions of public feeling which are unpredictable except to a genius. Ever since the arrival of Dr. Livingstone's last letter, two and a half years before, everyone had been content to take the Society's word for it that the Doctor was all right. Now, quite unexpectedly, they changed their minds, and the cause of this reversal was the news about Mirambo and Captain Burton's analysis of it which appeared in the papers the next day.

The genial way in which Burton had dismissed the danger annoyed the public, and his statement that the siege of Tabora would make no difference to Livingstone struck them as being absolute nonsense. All the Doctor's supplies went through Tabora, and if it was beleaguered by a gang of bandits, it was obvious that not a bale of anything would reach him. Overnight the whole country decided that the talk about Livingstone's safety had gone on long enough, and that it was high time something more definite was done about him.

The fact was that, as the months had gone by, and then one year, and then another, without a single word of authentic news, more and more people had become critical of the Society's attitude of *laissez-faire*. The Society's continued inaction now in the face of a clear threat from Mirambo tipped 'the balance. It seemed to the public that Livingstone was certainly in danger and might easily be dead, and the only thing the Society had done about it was to spend the evening talking about extinct volcanoes in Syria.

"I must confess", wrote *An Old Traveller* to *The Times*, referring to Dr. Livingstone,[5] "I am getting quite weary of hearing about the supposed safety of that distinguished traveller, especially from reports communicated at almost every meeting of the Geographical Society from Dr. Kirk at Zanzibar. For the last two years we have heard nothing but rumours founded on reports received at the British Agency at Zanzibar through Arab traders, and yet not one of these travellers has managed to bring down a line from Dr. Livingstone to assure us of his safety or even to tell us that he had seen him, but merely that somebody had informed someone else that the 'white traveller' had been seen by somebody!"

These sentiments exactly summed up the feelings of a large section of the public, and Sir Henry Rawlinson was quick to see the justice of their argument and to realize that unless he did something the Society would be in for a storm.

At the next meeting a fortnight later, on the 11th of December, he explained to the members that on further consideration he had come to the conclusion that Livingstone was in more danger than at first supposed. In view of this, and in view also of the extreme public concern which had shown itself, he felt it was the Society's clear duty to take some definite steps to find out what the position really was. One of the members had suggested that several messengers ought to be sent independently to try to make contact with Livingstone, to receive a hundred guineas reward if any one of them returned with a letter in the Doctor's own handwriting. Alternatively, the Society might deal with the situation more seriously and send out a full-scale expedition at once under some competent European. Sir Henry proposed putting both these suggestions to the Foreign Office for final choice, since Livingstone was a consul and was technically under their jurisdiction. Whichever the decision, the Society would carry it out, for it must never be said that they fell short of their responsibilities or failed their members in time of trouble.[6]

Four days later, on the 15th of December, Sir Henry wrote a letter to Dr. Kirk telling him of developments at home. This letter still exists, and gives an interesting and exact picture of the situation as it was at that moment, a fortnight before Christmas, a time which was seen afterwards to be critical, and during which many things were in the balance.

"Dear Dr. Kirk [wrote Sir Henry].[7] The information recently furnished by you as to renewed disturbances at Tabora [8] and the subsequent interruption of Mr. Stanley's journey into the interior has caused us much disquietude in the Geographical Council. We have now addressed the Foreign Office, suggesting that instructions be at once sent out to you to make every effort to communicate with Dr. Livingstone, either by special messengers or through the merchants trading with Manyema, and in the event of all such efforts proving ineffectual, we are seriously considering the question of despatching another expedition for the express purpose of positively ascertaining the Doctor's whereabouts, for there is no concealing the fact that a general belief is gaining ground, in which however I do not participate, that he is no longer living and that the Arab merchants designedly conceal his death.

"If Mr. Stanley gives up his journey to the Lake, do you think that Mr. Wakefield who is at Mombas would undertake to head a small expedition to Ujiji, or if necessary to Manyema? *Coute qu'il coute*, we MUST get positive information whether Livingstone is alive or dead, so do pray make a great effort to accomplish this."

This letter put the situation in a nutshell. Rather against their wills, the members of the Society were being pushed into action. There was a public outcry, and something had to be done about it. But the majority of them thought the fuss was rather unnecessary and that it was more than likely that Dr. Livingstone was well and in no danger whatsoever.

Six days after Sir Henry had written this letter, the first of Stanley's despatches from Tabora arrived in the *Herald* Offices in New York, and Bennett decided it would now be safe to tell the world the dramatic news that he intended to rescue Dr. Livingstone. Accordingly he released it in huge headlines across five complete columns of the *New York Herald* for the 22nd of December.

Nine days after this, on New Year's Day, 1872, Sir Henry Rawlinson in London announced his intention of rescuing Dr. Livingstone too, having just heard from the Foreign Office[9] that he would receive their full support if he launched an expedition, and having decided that it would be better to do so at once rather than wait for the doubtful return of a native messenger. Sir Henry did not know of Bennett's expedition, and Bennett could not have known of Sir Henry's and for at least a fortnight after the announcement of each, the one necessarily remained in ignorance of the other, since the mails took a minimum of two weeks to cross the Atlantic. In neither case was any advance news sent over by cable.

The reaction in New York to Bennett's announcement was surprising. It was greeted with roars of laughter, nobody believed a word of it, and it created so little stir that the correspondent of *The Times*, writing a long despatch on that day from Philadelphia, ignored it entirely.[10] The New Yorkers were always having their legs pulled by the papers, and they were extremely wary of a report of anything unusual. They had never forgotten the time in 1835 when the entire nation had been deceived about the discovery of life on the moon. A story was concocted by Richard Adams Locke a reporter on the *New York Sun* who said he had just read it in the *Edinburgh Journal of Science*, a journal which, in fact, was defunct. The writer in the journal had come back from an interview with the famous astronomer, Sir William Herschel, in South Africa. He had peeped through Sir William's new telescope, had seen the moon as though at a distance of eighty yards, and observed the most startling lunar creatures. There were miniature red-haired men with translucent wings, two-legged beavers from whose houses came puffs of smoke, and bearded unicorns with overhanging eyebrows like tennis-shades.

On this occasion with the *Herald*, however, the New Yorkers thought they could easily see through a little tale about Dr. Livingstone, and they refused to accept it for an instant. All Bennett's competitors derided it, and the most popular counter story was that Stanley was writing the whole thing from an hotel in the city. He was locked in his room, surrounded by books on Africa, and not allowed to look out of the window, in case he should be seen and recognized by a friend in the street, but in compensation for this imprisonment he was living on the best of everything. The only mystery was how he had managed to invent such realistic names as Mpwapwa and Wagogo—his first despatch from Tabora had been published in full, and it was crammed with the most authentic savage detail imaginable.

The announcement in England of Sir Henry Rawlinson's expedition, on the other hand, was received with satisfaction and excitement. It was romantic to picture a special force of intrepid Englishmen hastening into the twilit jungle to rescue the famous old explorer, and everyone's imagination was set on fire. Sir Henry Rawlinson was widely praised for the good sense of his decision, and he naturally felt pleased with himself for having vindicated the honour of the Society. He got down to the preparations at once, launched a public appeal for money, set up subscription committees in all the principal towns, opened the fund on the Society's behalf with £500, and asked the Treasury if they would contribute a similar amount. Money came pouring in immediately from places as far away as Sweden and Italy, and young men eagerly volunteered from all parts of the country.

When the news of Bennett's expedition arrived, it struck Sir Henry like a thunderclap. It was one thing to offer a stray young American a hearty welcome if he happened to see Dr. Livingstone in the course of a visit to Ujiji and bring back news of him; it was quite another to find that he was the emissary of a man who had deliberately sent him off to Africa to interfere with Britain's greatest living explorer, for whose welfare Sir Henry was himself responsible. All members of the Society were furious, and doubly enraged to find that the instigator was the notorious James Gordon Bennett, who was known to loathe the British and could not possibly care whether Livingstone was alive or dead. The whole thing was obviously just a stunt to increase the sale of his newspaper and make more money for himself.

Nobody could blame the Society for feeling like this, but Sir Henry Rawlinson went further and lost his head. His judgement went to the winds, and he now goaded everyone with frenzy to get his expedition away so that it could reach Africa and set off before Stanley could escape from Tabora. At all costs, regardless of appearances, he was determined to rescue Dr. Livingstone before Stanley, to save the honour of the Society, and once and for all to put James Gordon Bennett in his place.

Stanley, personally, was not considered at this point, for he was, after all, only the agent of the mogul who had sent him. But doubtless when the Society's expedition had brushed Mirambo aside, reached Ujiji, and succoured Livingstone, its leader would spare a few moments to think of the young American. As one of the members of the Society said,[11] once you had a European in charge of an expedition of this kind, African travel became easy. The young Mr. Stanley with the pathetic remnants of his expensive force could be rescued in a few hours. This was a little errand to which Sir Henry looked forward with a certain grim joy.

The history of the Livingstone Search and Relief Expedition

of 1872 is a story of muddle, blindness, jealousy, and enthusiasm. The Foreign Office supported it, but the Treasury refused to subscribe to it. The Admiralty agreed to provide arms
and ammunition for it, but would not allow full pay to the
officers who took part in it. Many responsible people felt it was
pointless, in view of Bennett's expedition, and just for this
reason Sir Henry Rawlinson determined to push on with it at
all costs. The public as a whole thought Sir Henry might as
well keep going, as it was rather fun to have a race with the
Americans, and it would make the Doctor's rescue all the more
certain.

> "I send you my little mite for Dr. Livingstone's search
> [wrote Florence Nightingale to Sir Henry Rawlinson]. May
> God speed every effort to save one of the greatest men of our
> time, or, if he is dead, to save his discoveries! If it cost
> £10,000 to send him a pair of boots, England ought to give
> it. But England provides the great men, and then England
> leaves them to perish." [12]

This was exactly what everybody felt, and when the letter
was read at a meeting it was received with acclamation. The
public had been incensed by the Treasury's refusal to help and
by their excuse that there was no precedent for giving public
money to private committees, and everyone determined to
show the Chancellor of the Exchequer that they could manage
perfectly well without him. At the end of a few weeks the fund
had risen to almost £5,000.

After much excitement and a great many speeches the expedition sailed on the 9th of February on the "Abydos", a ship which
happened to be sailing direct to Zanzibar on that date and on
which the party were given a free passage, the only piece of
luck they had. From more than two hundred volunteers, a
naval lieutenant called Llewellyn Dawson was chosen as leader.
He was a trained surveyor, twenty-five years old, with previous
experience of exploration in China and South America. The

DR. LIVINGSTONE

second in command was William Henn, a red-haired Irishman, also aged twenty-five, who was without experience, but had a good name for reliability. The third member was Oswell Livingstone, the second son of the Doctor, who had broken off his medical studies at Glasgow University to join. He was only twenty years old and in poor health, and it turned out afterwards that he only wanted to see his father to get some money out of him.

They left Wapping Basin on a clear morning just after noon, fully equipped in every detail with arms and ammunition, tents, tropical clothing, instruments, and maps. They had also a carefully chosen assortment of gifts for native chiefs to the value of £158 14s. 3d.,[13] the most valuable of which was an "elegant silver tray and coffee-pot" for the Sultan of Zanzibar. On arrival they hoped to enlist a thirty-two-year-old missionary, the Rev. Charles New from Mombasa, who had been in Africa many years and would act as interpreter. Six English-speaking African native boys had been requested from the Nassick missionary school at Bombay to be sent direct to Zanzibar as bearers. All other arrangements had been left to Dr. Kirk, who had been ordered by cable to recruit a native guard of fifty men, and to get ready the usual quantities of cloth and beads.

The only things the members of the expedition failed to have with them were proper orders. They had instructions about communications, expenses, chain of command, and what they were to do if Livingstone wanted to be left alone or brought home with them. They had been given written copies of these, and had signed them to confirm that they understood them. But on the subject of Stanley and a possible meeting with him, in the presence of the Doctor or not, they had no orders whatsoever, and there was not a single mention or implication[14] of Stanley in anything that was said to them. He might as well have been searching for Livingstone on the moon. Sir Henry Rawlinson, who wrote the orders, ignored his existence completely, and nobody had dared speak of him or ask what the expedition should do if it met him.

On the very day the party reached the mainland[15] of Africa at Bagamoyo, three of Stanley's men arrived with the news of his success, and a week later Stanley arrived himself. It fell to William Henn to welcome him, since Llewellyn Dawson had lost his temper and resigned when he heard the news, and it was William Henn whom Stanley first saw on reaching Bagamoyo —the young man with reddish whiskers who came out of the large white house and congratulated him. To Henn's credit, he did not disillusion Stanley on the first evening with the news of the jealousy in England, and Stanley went to bed in exalted spirits, believing he had achieved his ambition at last and that from now on he would be respected, taken seriously, and treated as an equal by all the people who had snubbed him in the past—the cornets of the Scinde Horse, the English news-paper-men, and the silent officials like Dr. Kirk.

He records that he lay awake for a long time that night, un-used to the soft mattress and the clean blankets, wondering if the past fourteen months had been really true. He thought of the welcome that might await him in England: a public re-ception, perhaps, speeches, congratulations, popularity. He lay smiling to himself in the darkness, his mind full of dreams, and it was past three o'clock before he fell asleep.

Chapter Fifteen

THE next day Stanley sailed over to Zanzibar and met Llewellyn Dawson, who congratulated him without much enthusiasm. Stanley was taken aback by such half-heartedness, but Dawson was so annoyed by the way everything had turned out that he could hardly control himself. In excuse he told Stanley the full story of the Relief Expedition, and all about his own personal troubles at Zanzibar. The hurricane had blown away his accounts. The arrival of Stanley's men had caused him to retire. The missionary from Mombasa, Charles New, had refused to serve under William Henn, and had retired also. Henn was young enough to be his baby brother, he said. Henn had behaved with complete frivolity and had only thought about big-game hunting. He had been enchanted at Stanley's success because it relieved him of any further worry and gave him hopes of a safari. He had never been in Africa before, and he had a great ambition to bag a zebra.

Stanley listened to all these tales with astonishment. He was annoyed to find that Dawson was not pleased to see him, and he retaliated by giving him a stiff lecture. Dawson ought never to have given up his leadership of the Relief Expedition on the strength of a few native rumours. If he was going to do it at all, he should have waited until Stanley arrived himself with the facts. After all, the whole report might have been a myth.

This rebuke was more than Dawson could stand, and he took umbrage and wished Stanley good morning.

The next day Dr. Kirk, the British consul, called to congratulate Stanley, and he did so with admiration and warmth, Kirk was delighted that Livingstone had been found, both from the point of view of an old friend and as the Government official responsible for him. He bore Stanley no ill feeling, and in fact as soon as he had discovered the true purpose of Stanley's

133

expedition he had sent a letter after him asking him to take charge of any supplies for Livingstone which he might come across. Kirk felt that all the fuss about Livingstone had been unnecessary, for he had always believed Livingstone was all right; Stanley's return would now put an end to it.

Although Stanley was rather non-committal about the Doctor, he gave Kirk two personal letters, and Kirk went away quite satisfied, content to let him fill the gaps later, when he felt like it. Kirk knew the truth about Stanley's expedition by this time, and realized that Stanley was under orders and might have to hold back a good deal of news until he had sent it off to the *Herald*.

But it was now Dr. Kirk's turn to become embroiled and to lose his temper. Livingstone was an old friend of many years' standing, but the letters he now read from him were peremptory, and might have been addressed to a junior official. Neither of them contained anything but complaints about the way he had been neglected, about the fact that useless slaves had been sent up with his goods instead of reliable freemen, and about the immense length of time everything had taken to reach him. ". . . I see that you are under the impression that goods . . . reach Ujiji in about a month. . . ."[16] The box packed by you was about four years on the way." As a final insult, Kirk was instructed to hand over £500 to Stanley with the implication that the next caravan might be sent up by someone who would give proper attention to its despatch.

Dr. Kirk was absolutely furious at this. He was certain that Stanley had put Livingstone up to it as a piece of anti-British mischief-making, and although he handed over the money, he swore it was the last thing he would ever do for Livingstone, except on direct orders from the Foreign Office.

Every kind of recrimination and retort now flew about the island. Kirk called Livingstone a "damned old scoundrel",[17] and the Rev. Charles New overheard him and was deeply shocked, and determined to report him to Sir Henry Rawlinson. Henn accused Stanley of trying to prevent his going forward with the Relief Expedition up to Tabora, and Stanley replied primly that for Livingstone's sake he must speak the truth—a young, apple-cheeked youth of Henn's experience would be an encumbrance to any explorer. Henn was huffed and vowed that, so far as he was concerned, the Relief Expedition could go to the devil. Livingstone's son, who so far had managed to keep out of trouble, felt so humiliated at his father's letters that he resigned also. He was "disgusted and ashamed" he said.[18] In consequence he received a talk from Stanley on filial piety. It was true that he would be a nuisance to his father at Tabora, but the path of duty was clear, and he had no right to deny his ageing parent the joy of an unexpected jungle reunion.

By the 10th of May, only three days after Stanley had arrived, not a single member of the Relief Expedition had a word to say for him except that he was the most villainous bounder they had ever met. Dr. Kirk had brooded over his insults so much that he had become unbalanced about them, and had written to the Foreign Office in the wildest terms:[19] Stanley got hold of other letters from the Doctor which he was suppressing so that no one else should have any information; he had opened Dr. Kirk's letters and read them, for he knew their contents even to the very phrases and expressions; he had got round Livingstone to such an extent that the latter had promised to go to America when he came out—an event which, Dr. Kirk remarked acidly, "I am now glad to think is not likely to be for three years".

These accusations against Stanley were mainly false, but at the same time there was a modicum of truth in the general implication that he had stirred up Livingstone's temper. Livingstone had felt certain, long before he had met Stanley, that Kirk had been neglecting him, but Stanley's arrival had seemed to prove it. While they had been together at Ujiji, Stanley had received eleven packets of letters, but Livingstone had continued to receive nothing. Stanley had been snubbed by Kirk and had been glad to get his own back by telling tales about him. He had told Livingstone that Kirk thought him tiresome, and also that it was high time he came home and left the discovery of the source of the Nile to somebody younger. So far as Livingstone was concerned this remark had confirmed all his suspicions and showed that Kirk had betrayed him.[20] The trouble was that both Stanley and Livingstone had a grievance against Kirk independently long before they met. When they did so, and found they had identical opinions about him, Kirk stood no chance of appearing innocent.

This was exceptionally bad luck for Dr. Kirk, because in fact he was one of the most hard-working and successful civil servants of his generation, and had always been an admirer of Livingstone's and was one of his truest friends. An official inquiry the next year showed beyond doubt that nothing but a series of unpredictable misfortunes had kept Livingstone without supplies for such a long time, and that Kirk had always done his best for him.

But of all this Stanley knew and cared nothing. When Kirk became stiff with him, as he did the moment he opened the Doctor's letters, Stanley saw red. He swore that the British and American public should know about Kirk's laziness, and that he would publish it at the first opportunity to the four quarters of the globe. The *Herald* would print it, and the *Herald* had the largest circulation of any paper in the world.

By the end of the month Stanley had disbanded the *Herald* Expedition paid all outstanding accounts with Arab merchants, and was ready to leave for home. He had collected together the party of men he had promised to send back to Livingstone, and had made every possible arrangement to ensure that they reached him. Twenty-five of his own men had joined it, six others were the English-speaking native boys who had been sent over from Bombay for the Relief Expedition, and the remainder were chosen by Stanley himself from volunteers on the island. He had managed to acquire all the stores and equipment the Doctor had asked for, and as extra presents he sent a bottle of champagne and a plum pudding.

"Permit me to wish you joy of your plum pudding [he wrote in a last letter to the Doctor on the 25th of May].[21] And now, my dear and good friend, I have done to the utmost of my ability what I have promised. . . . All I can now, is to wish you the blessing of God, and the beneficent Providence who has watched over you so long."

He sent the party off under the supervision of the interpreter of the American consulate on the 27th of May, and the following morning he boarded the steamer "Africa", which he had chartered from the German consulate for $900. Selim and Kalulu were with him, and also Oswell Livingstone, Henn, and New. Dawson had left already, having refused to travel in the same ship with him, and had sailed earlier for the Cape of Good Hope. Stanley's plan was to catch a homeward-bound French mail-steamer at the Seychelles, and if he succeeded he would be at Aden within a fortnight, and in London by the end of June.

The air was clear and the sun dazzling as the "Africa" ran up the Zanzibar Channel, and in the extreme distance could be seen the outline of the mainland at Bagamoyo. But Stanley did not look at it, not bothering about the past, but absorbed in speculations about the future. The ship began to roll abominably, and he went forward to the bows and watched the sea.

The "Africa" missed the mail-boat at the Seychelles by twelve hours, and as the next steamer did not arrive for a month the whole party was forced to wait for it. Henn went off by himself to the Phœnix Hotel because he had had a further humiliating quarrel with Stanley and never wished to speak to him again. Oswell Livingstone and the Reverend New had become quite friendly with Stanley, however, and they all three rented a bungalow on the outskirts of Victoria which they named "Livingstone Cottage".[22] The delay was annoying, but

they determined to make the best of it, and they called on the
Civil Commissioner, Hales Franklyn, and were asked to dinner
with him, and went for excursions and picnics in the surrounding countryside, had their photographs taken, and finished up
by enjoying themselves thoroughly, Stanley, especially, was
glad of the rest, and they were all quite sorry when the steamer
arrived at last.

"We have had an extremely pleasant month here and I feel
quite melancholy at leaving," Oswell Livingstone wrote to Dr.
Kirk. "Stanley, New . . . and myself . . . have got on first
rate." [23]

They left Mahe on the 6th of July, four days later they arrived at Aden, and from then on there were no more delays.

Stanley's first full report of the meeting with Livingstone
had been published a week earlier in every important paper
in the world, and even at Aden he found himself a celebrity.
There were instructions awaiting him and a personal message
from Bennett, "You are now famous as Livingstone, having
discovered the discoverer. Accept my thanks, and whole
world." [24] At Marseilles Stanley was to meet Dr. Hosmer, the
Herald London agent, and hand over to him the two letters
which Livingstone had written to Bennett. They would be
telegraphed to New York, regardless of cost, to allow Stanley
to keep a promise to deliver them before any others. There
was a cable from Hosmer, too, ". . . more splendid achievement, energetic devotion, and generous gallantry not in history of human endeavour". [25]

By the 15th of July Stanley was at Suez, and he reached Mar-
silles on the evening of the 24th. It was past midnight when the
ship berthed, but he went ashore at once, and at two o'clock,
after a search, found Dr. Hosmer in an hotel, in bed and fast
asleep. He flung open the door and woke him up.

"Who is it?" asked Dr. Hosmer sleepily.

The other, in a voice that trembled with excitement, answered simply, "MR. STANLEY!!"

The next day he went on to Paris, and the moment he arrived he was besieged by journalists from every major paper in Europe. There was the greatest curiosity in the capital, and every kind of rumour circulated about him. The Paris Geographical Society met to consider the situation and decided that he was an impostor. *Le Soir* said he was Lord Stanley, son of the Early of Derby, and *Le Figaro* said he was nobody, and a fraud. Other journals quoted the *Carnarvon Herald*, that he was a Welshman called John Rowlands from Denbigh whose mother kept an inn at St. Asaph, and Stanley himself denied this and told a special correspondent from the *Daily Telegraph* that he was an American, "pur sang". He began to give away too many of his adventures to other newspapers, and he received a furious telegram of two words from Bennett: "STOP TALKING." He was invited to breakfast with General Sherman and Monckton Milnes by the United States Minister, Mr. Washburne. An American publisher offered him $50,000 for the exclusive rights of a book.

He stayed in Paris for six days, and on the night before he left, the American colony gave a farewell banquet in his honour at the Hotel Chatham. The new dining-room of the hotel was "tastefully fitted up for the occasion", and there were nearly a hundred guests. As it was a hot night, all the windows were wide open, and a further large crowd stood outside in the courtyard and gazed at him. Mr. Washburne was in the chair, and every distinguished American in Paris was in attendance.

In presenting Stanley to the guests, Mr. Washburne spoke of his tremendous journey to Ujiji and the incredible difficulties he had overcome. Stanley's introduction to Livingstone and the old man's brief reply would never be forgotten and must surely "become historical". To take the words of Sir Walter Scott in Marmion, it had indeed been a case of "On, Stanley, on!"

Stanley answered simply, relating first the already well-known interview with Bennett in the Grand Hotel, then speaking with warmth and admiration of Livingstone, and finally coming to an end with a violent attack on Dr. Kirk, whom, he said, he had been given a mission by Livingstone to expose as a traitor.

According to *The Times*, everyone was struck by "the extreme simplicity and modesty of his bearing", and although his passionate remarks on Dr. Kirk caused some uneasiness, he received a tumultuous ovation.

There were more speeches by other guests. A Mr. Young told the first of many stories in parody of Bennett's instructions. Bennett, he said, was on his yacht, and Stanley was standing beside him on the deck.

"Mr. Stanley, do you believe in the great sea-serpent?"

"I do, sir."

"Then go and find him. You can have unlimited credit. Twist a cable about his jaws, tow him in from the sea, and beach him upon the spit of Sandy Hook."

Kalulu, whom Stanley had brought back with him as a page, was led in and placed on a chair, wearing the *kepi* of a French captain. He was dressed in a jacket and trousers and patent-leather boots, and carried a red velvet purse with gilt embroidery which someone had given him on the train from Marseilles. He behaved like a perfect gentleman, although his clothes appeared to annoy him. The ladies outside in the courtyard beyond the dining-room were ecstatic at his appearance, and when he came out several of them rushed forward and kissed him.

There were more speeches, much laughter and hilarity, a good many cigars and glasses of brandy, and it was past one o'clock before everyone went to bed. Stanley sat through it all slightly in a daze. Everything that he had dreamed of had become reality. Even the chef had honoured him. A sumptuous dish of succulent chicken and truffles had been prepared, a special creation with a new name—his name: "*Poularde truffée à la Stanley*". All through dinner his eye kept catching the words on the menu, and he found himself reading them over and over again.

Chapter Sixteen

DURING all this time, while Stanley had been at Zanzibar and the Seychelles, Sir Henry Rawlinson had not been idle in England. There had been silence from Africa for a short period after the departure of his expedition, and then word had come that Livingstone had been found. Sir Henry was delighted. It so happened that he received a telegram with the news just as he was stepping out of his house in Charles Street [26] one evening to go to a banquet of the Geographical Society, and he put the message in his pocket and hurried off. During the course of the proceedings he produced it with all the subtlety for which, as a master raconteur, he was famous. Livingstone was safe, he announced. They must all rejoice. Furthermore, the American, Mr. Stanley, was safe also, heroically rescued by Dr. Livingstone. In spite of the fact that Sir Henry's telegram actually read, "Dr. Livingstone is safe with Stanley",[27] Sir Henry knew it must be the other way round. This was evident because Livingstone had always been perfectly safe at Ujiji, and abundantly supplied, whereas Stanley was known to have been trapped by Mirambo and robbed of everything. It was clear, therefore, that Livingstone had managed to reach Tabora and relieve him.

In spite of Sir Henry's reputation for scientific accuracy, there was some confusion when he said this, and he clarified it at a meeting of the Geographical Society on the 13th of May.

"There is one point on which a little *éclaircissement* is desirable, because a belief seems to prevail that Mr. Stanley has discovered and relieved Dr. Livingstone; whereas, without any disparagement to Mr. Stanley's energy, activity, and loyalty, if there has been any discovery and relief it is Dr. Livingstone who has discovered and relieved Mr. Stanley. Dr.

Livingstone, indeed, is in clover, while Mr. Stanley is nearly destitute. . . . It is only proper that the relative position of the parties should be correctly stated." [28]

There were many people who could hardly believe their ears when they heard these remarks, especially in view of Sir Henry's appeal at Christmas for the Relief Expedition, when Livingstone was said to be on the brink of death, and for three years without a single bale of cloth or string of beads or bottle of medicine.

But Sir Henry stuck to his guns and repeated his theory on the 27th of May and again on the 24th of June. He was gratified to think how pleased Livingstone must have been to rescue the struggling American journalist.

The first full report from Africa arrived on the 3rd of July, a long despatch from Stanley himself with the news of the meeting at Ujiji, given to the English Press by the *New York Herald*.

Sir Henry Rawlinson was silenced by this, but other members of the Geographical Society came to his rescue and threw cold water on it. They warned the public not to believe everything that appeared in the newspapers, and pointed out that many of Livingstone's geographical theories as quoted in the despatch were nonsense, though doubtless this was only due to Stanley's weak memory. In private they all agreed with a Mr. Stone of Doncaster, who wrote to *The Times* saying that he doubted the entire report. He drew attention to the fact that Livingstone was described as "pale-looking". Everyone knew he was sunburnt the colour of dark mahogany, and this surely proved the whole story was an invention.

These quibblings were too much for the public and they attacked the Geographers openly.

"Pray allow me to suggest to . . . Sir Henry Rawlinson and the Geographical Society [wrote a Mr. Fiske, voicing a general opinion] that a very proper subject for discussion would be what honours are most appropriate to be paid to Mr. Stanley on his arrival here." [29]

But the Geographical Society was damned if it was going to give honours to anybody, and all the members refused to consider it.

Finally, when Stanley arrived in Paris, a rumour began to circulate in London that Sir Henry Rawlinson was going to call an extraordinary meeting of the Society to welcome him and consider Livingstone's discoveries. Sir Henry wrote to *The Times* to deny it, saying that none of Livingstone's despatches received up to date contained anything geographical, and therefore there was nothing to discuss. There was no hurry, but if anything did transpire it could be heard by the Geographical Section of the British Association, which met at Brighton in a fortnight's time.

"All this, we fear, conceals a certain chagrin to which [30] Sir Henry Rawlinson . . . ought not to give way," commented the *Daily Telegraph*.

But Sir Henry was not in the habit of changing his plans for the penny newspapers, and he stuck to his normal arrangements for August, and went down to the country. Apart from anything else, there was a heat-wave in London with temperatures over 95 degrees, and the airless streets were positively suffocating.

Stanley arrived in England on the 1st of August, and all his dreams of civic receptions and official welcomes were blown to the winds. He reached Dover in high spirits, still musing on the toasts and speeches of the banquet in Paris the night before, and was met only by two poor relations from Denbigh who failed to recognize him. In London no one from any official quarter came near him, and he learnt from the newspapers that according to the latest rumour he had never been within a thousand miles of Livingstone but had simply acquired his diary and letters by robbery. He had met a native carrying them to the coast and had stolen them and brought them home himself. The story of the meeting at Ujiji was just a lie to explain his possession of the letters. Finally, he picked up *The Times* and read Sir Henry Rawlinson's announcement and realized that the Geographers had no intention of welcoming him at all.

These first hours in London brought Stanley the most bitter disillusion of his life. He had been warned in Paris of the jealousy of the Geographical Society, but he had been too excited to take much notice of it, and also jealousy was a failing he did not understand, any more than he understood other sentiments which were absent from his nature, such as moral weakness or fear. He simply could not believe that the Geographers would grudge his achievement, any more than he believed that Sir Henry Rawlinson had said that he, Stanley, had been rescued by Livingstone. These things were beyond his imagination. Life to him was hard but straightforward. You did something well, and you were praised for it, and when this took place on a high political level with the rescue of a national hero, the nation, naturally, gave you some sort of official thanks. This was a principle equivalent to justice itself.

But in applying this principle he failed entirely to take into account the frightful humiliation caused by Sir Henry Rawlinson, and the extraordinary speculation and confusion that Sir Henry's behaviour had aroused.

If Sir Henry had acknowledged Stanley from the first, none of these difficulties would have arisen. Since he had not done so, and since he was a man of public standing, a number of people thought that perhaps he was right. They felt that no one in his senses would commit himself in such a way unless he was certain of his facts and, therefore, surely all that he said was true. The bad reputation of the *New York Herald* added to these doubts, for it was impossible to be sure of anything Bennett ever printed, and for weeks after Stanley arrived a minority continued to suspect the whole affair was a hoax. This suspicion was further inspired by the two letters of thanks which Livingstone had written to Bennett, and which were published. Their style was odd and journalistic, quite unlike anything Livingstone normally wrote, and they contained quotations from American poets which Livingstone might not have known. Altogether they gave the impression that Stanley had written them, and this, in fact, was half correct, for Stanley had helped Livingstone to draft them to make them more suitable for the American public.

The disappointment and unhappiness of these first days in England affected Stanley for the rest of his career. "All the actions of my life, and I may say all my thoughts since 1872, have been strongly coloured by the storm of abuse . . . about me then," he wrote thirty years later in his autobiography. He was dumbfounded by the lack of official recognition and by all the jealousies, mean rumours, and accusations. He felt they proved, once and for all, that mankind was against him, and that nothing he could do would ever be right. In these few days he remembered and suffered again all the bitterness of his early childhood, and it crystallized into a consuming resentment against life itself.

He became "a perfect Ishmaelite, with his hand against every man, and feeling every man's hand was raised against him",[31] said a friend and contemporary. Stanley reckoned afterwards that it took twelve years to live down all the scandals and lies that were spread about him at this time, and he never forgave Sir Henry Rawlinson for starting them. At this moment in his life his character finally set. All hopes of praise or gentleness were crushed, and they were never allowed to influence him again.

But in addition to all this he was also upset by his friends— the journalists who admired and the public who cheered him. They slapped him on the back, but they laughed at him. Whenever he came into a room they got up, held out their hands, and greeted him as he had greeted Livingstone. They smiled and bowed and said, "Mr. Stanley, I presume?"

In many ways this made the deepest hurt of all. When he thought of the person to whom he had used this expression—Dr. Livingstone, a great man who had loved and understood him—he was stung to the roots of his being. Anyone who said it to him received such a flash from his smouldering grey eyes that they never contemplated saying it again. But there was no means of stamping it out. There were jokes about it on the very day it appeared in the papers, and overnight it became a by-word. Even when he tried to explain in "How I Found Livingstone" how normal it was for Anglo-Saxons to greet each other in ways rather like this, no one took any notice of him.[32] The expression had passed into the language long before he arrived in Europe, and there was nothing to be done.

"Dr. Livingstone, I presume?" said one dummy to another in a men's fashion plate in the October issue of the *Tailor & Cutter*; "Dr. Livingstone, I presume?" shouted a host of clowns and funny men in the music-halls, dressed up in black tights and woolly wigs; "Dr. Livingstone, I presume?" murmured the old gentlemen to each other in the soft crannies of their clubs. There was no escape from it or denying it. The only person who avoided it was Sir Henry Rawlinson. Nobody dared presume anything about Dr. Livingstone to him.

In spite of the attitude of the Geographers, however, the public at large thought Stanley's return extremely romantic, and his arrival in the capital caused one of the greatest excitements ever recorded in the United Kingdom. "I have seldom, if ever, known anything create so widespread and intense an interest throughout the country," wrote the eminent Quaker, J. B. Braithwaite, to Dr. Livingstone a few weeks afterwards. "It is impossible to describe the sensation thy letters have produced and the interest that has been awakened." [33]

The office of the *New York Herald* in Fleet Street was besieged by journalists asking about Stanley, and in the first week of August every newspaper in the country carried articles about him. The Foreign Office, too, as Livingstone's Government de-

HENRY M. STANLEY, 1872

partment, was bombarded by questions from friends and advice from cranks. A Mr. Franklyn Coxworthy, who explained there was electricity in the earth's crust in Africa pointed out to the Foreign Secretary that England had been humiliated by the *Herald*, and the only way to recover her position in the world was to offer to pay for Stanley's expedition and send Bennett £10,000. A Mr. Joshua Ambrose, in a very long and inky memorandum, warned Lord Granville about the dangers of international incidents. Stanley had flown the Stars and Stripes beside the Union Jack over the waters of Lake Tanganyika. England must take care! [34]

Stanley was inundated with letters too, and in one post alone he had twenty-eight invitations from people he had never heard of. Sir Bartle Frere, Sir Charles Dilke, Lady Franklin, Baroness Burdett Coutts, and many other important and well-known people asked him to their houses, and the Anglo-American Press gave a dinner for him at the Garrick Club, attended by every important journalist in London. Madame Tussaud's waxworks sent an artist to model him, and exhibited him with Kalulu, shaking hands with Dr. Livingstone at Ujiji, all three dressed in clothes identical with those worn at the time of the meeting. The London Stereoscopic Company of Regent Street advertised Stanley's photograph, with or without Kalulu, post free for a shilling. Emrik and Binger of Holborn Viaduct issued a coloured lithograph of a group of Arabs and natives watching Stanley and Livingstone shaking hands, and thousands of tradesmen sent this out as their Christmas calendar. The well-known water-colour artist, Orlando Norrie, was also moved by the drama of the meeting and painted a picture of it. But he got into a muddle over the circumstances, and drew the two men on camels, with Livingstone under an umbrella.

But in spite of all these acknowledgments, there were still a number of people who were not convinced. Several papers continued to publish libellous articles about Stanley, and Mark Twain, who happened to be in London, added to the confusion by saying that *he* had found Livingstone, although, as an old friend, he did not mind Stanley taking the credit for it. Stanley was forced to ask Livingstone's family to certify that the diary and correspondence were authentic. They did so, and he published their letters in *The Times*. He made the same request to Lord Granville with regard to some official despatches from Livingstone, and Lord Granville also wrote to him, generously saying that he had no idea, until Stanley mentioned it, that there were any doubts about them. This letter Stanley published in the papers too.

With the publication of Lord Granville's letter it was impossible for Sir Henry Rawlinson to ignore Stanley any longer, and at the end of the first week of August he returned from the country and called a meeting of the Geographical Society. All that Stanley claimed was now proved, and Sir Henry sent him an official letter of congratulation, excusing himself and the Society for the delay in doing so, and asking him to address the British Association the following week at Brighton.

Stanley accepted. He felt indifferent now whether any official body paid attention to him or not, but at the same time he was glad to have a chance to give a public account of his journey. He meant to show that quite apart from the finding of Livingstone he had done some original exploration himself. Most of the false rumours about him had died down, but the Geographers were now treating him with condescension, calling him a "Fancyographer", and saying that his march at such a speed with such a gigantic caravan was a new type of travel with which they were not well acquainted. It could hardly produce anything very scientific, and was more like a steeplechase than an expedition.

As far as Stanley could see, jungle travel was jungle travel, and he felt that he could discover new hills and rivers as well as anybody else. Two-thirds of his journey had been through country never before traversed by white man, and he hoped that when the Geographers realized this they would change their minds. He went down to Brighton on Wednesday the 14th, and was welcomed as the guest of the Corporation by special invitation of Dr. Burrowes, the Mayor.

The particular group before which Stanley was to speak was the Geographical Section of the Association, and this Section did not convene until the Friday—two days later. The meeting was held in the concert-room in Middle Street, a fine large hall over two hundred feet long, with a stage at one end and a gallery running round the sides. The floor was filled with rows of chairs, the front row having crimson cushions for distinguished guests. On the wall behind the stage was a huge map of Africa.

The meeting was due at eleven o'clock in the morning, but more than two hours before this time the forward places began to fill up, and by ten-thirty the entire hall was packed to capacity with a crowd of nearly three thousand people. The prospect of Stanley's first public appearance had been the main topic of conversation for days, and in particular many ladies were determined to see him and had come to the hall early. At ten forty-five a stir in the back of the room disclosed the arrival of the exiled Emperor Napoleon III with the Empress Eugénie and the Prince Imperial, but the crush was so great that they had difficulty in reaching their chairs in the front row. At ten-fifty the organizing committee felt there was no point in waiting longer, since every seat was taken, and Mr. Francis Galton the chairman, Sir Henry Rawlinson, the Mayor and Stanley appeared and mounted the platform. Stanley was presented to the Emperor, the chairman made a few opening remarks, including the observation that he hoped Stanley might tell them a little about himself to clear up certain mysteries, and Stanley himself stepped forward to speak. He appeared calm and determined, although inwardly he was extremely nervous. As he came forward to the rostrum he was greeted with an explosion of applause.

Stanley now made a fatal mistake, for instead of keeping to his prepared text, the title of which was "Discoveries at the

North End of Lake Tanganyika", he allowed himself to begin with an extempore account of his summons by Bennett and his whole journey to Ujiji. The British Association, an august body of distinguished professional men, expected to be addressed seriously with facts and figures, and without any flourishes. "The first task of a geographer", said one of them in this manner at a later meeting, "is to ascertain by observation, and to delineate by maps and descriptions, the forms and relative positions and characteristics of the various features of all the regions of the earth." [35]

After three false starts, Stanley began like this: "I consider myself in the light of a Troubadour, to relate to you the tale of an old man who is tramping onward to discover the source of the Nile."

Some of the Geographers smiled, but luckily Stanley did not see them. He spoke in this vein at some considerable length, of all his travels and experiences with Livingstone, and of his journey home. Finally, he turned on the chairman for asking personal questions about his origins which, he said, was nothing but nosey parkering.

The chairman ignored this attack, but reminded the audience that they were gathered together to hear facts, and not sensational stories, and that they ought now to examine Stanley's tale to discover the facts. In this spirit of scientific method he would like to ask him the first question. Would Stanley tell them about the water in Lake Tanganyika—was it sweet or brackish?

Stanley boiled at having his journey to Ujiji described as a sensational story. He felt that the chairman was trying to make a fool of him, and he determined to do the same to him in return.

The water of Lake Tanganyika was delicious, he said, the nicest in the world. There was one thing it was particularly good for, and that was making tea.

The audience laughed, and the chairman was forced to accept defeat and carry on with the meeting.

After this, the proceedings went as follows: First, a reading of those parts of Livingstone's despatches connected with his work and theories on the source of the Nile. Then a paper by the famous African traveller, Colonel Grant, a critical analysis of the geographical content of Livingstone's two letters to Bennett. Next, some remarks by a well-known geographer, Dr. Beke, proving (quite correctly as it turned out afterwards) that the river on which Livingstone was working was the Congo. Lastly, some words from Sir Henry Rawlinson saying much the same thing and also disclaiming any jealousy on the part of the Geographical Society. It was quite the other way round, he said. They were all delighted at Stanley's achievement, and as long ago as last November they had wished him success and promised him a hearty welcome if he came to England. After this, Stanley spoke again.

By this time he felt he had heard enough double talk from Sir Henry Rawlinson, on top of criticism of his own and Livingstone's discoveries, and he made no attempt not to say so.

"Colonel Grant says that Dr. Livingstone has made a mistake about the river Lualaba, but I want to know how a geographer resident in England can say there is no such river when Dr. Livingstone has seen it? Dr. Beke, living in London, and never having been within two thousand miles of the spot, declares positively that Livingstone has not discovered the source of the Nile, whereas Livingstone who has devoted thirty-five years to Africa only says he *thinks* he has discovered it. I think if a man goes there and says 'I have seen the source of the river," the man sitting in his easy chair or lying in bed cannot dispute this fact on any grounds of theory."

He then also attacked Sir Henry Rawlinson for drawing maps of Africa to suit his convenience, bowed to the Emperor, and sat down.

This was a little too much for the chairman, and he reminded the audience that very often a man at home had access to far more facts from maps and books than the explorer on the spot, even supposing the latter had found a few new ones. But all the same, whatever the direction of the system of drainage on which Livingstone had been working, they had all witnessed Stanley's passionate support of the Doctor's theories, and could draw their own conclusions. A formal resolution of thanks to Stanley was then proposed and was carried with acclamation.

So far as the Geographers were concerned, the meeting had been a disgraceful pantomime, but to the audience, nine-tenths of whom had come only to listen to Stanley and did not care in the least where the Nile originated, it had been a most entertaining success. The old professors who had sniffed at Stanley had seen their pride properly punctured, and serve them all right. From the public's point of view, it was Stanley who carried the day.

It has to be said, in fairness to the Geographers, that on this occasion it was not they who behaved badly, but Stanley. Four years later he himself was to find that Livingstone's river was the Congo and that all the Geographers had theorized was correct. Smarting from injustice, longing to make clear to the world how disgracefully Livingstone had been neglected, and how weary and unrewarding his explorations of the last six years had been, Stanley took any criticism of Livingstone as an insult, both to the old man and to himself. He had never expected his lecture to be the subject of discussion afterwards and he was quite unprepared for it. He spoke as a guest, and he expected to be heard without interruption, and thanked and allowed to go home. To have his remarks discussed, even in a friendly way, was equivalent to having them doubted. In spite of his success with the audience, he left the meeting feeling humiliated, and it convinced him once again that whatever he said, all the Geographers would be against him.

But the next night he fared worse, and suffered the final, pulverizing snub of all. It was in the Royal Pavilion, at a banquet of the Sussex Medical Society, and he was asked to reply to the toast, "The Visitors". Once again he spoke of Livingstone, in the same sincere but unexpected manner, but as he got under way he began to forget himself and was carried away in his mind to the jungle, as though he were talking to natives, and he started to wave his arms about and dramatize, and mimic the people he was describing. He was an odd little figure, standing in evening dress before the eighty white-shirted physicians, his jet hair falling over his round face, his piercing grey eyes glittering with emotion, his red cheeks glowing above his black limp moustache and wispy imperial beard, his American voice vibrating and lilting, his tremendous shoulders heaving in his newly-made tail coat that somehow refused to fit him.

This time the audience was composed entirely of professional men, and they began to look at each other and make faces. Finally one of them burst into a shattering guffaw. Stanley stopped as though he had been shot. He changed his tone, and with all the consuming bitterness that was in him, turned on them and lashed out.

Was it because he was an American that they dared to treat him like this? Did they themselves discover the origin of a patient before they healed him? Had Dr. Livingstone asked his nationality before he had welcomed him? Enough insults and sneers had been thrown at him the day before, and theirs, now, pushed him beyond the limit of his endurance.

Before anyone knew what had happened, Stanley had marched out of the room.

A week later he wrote to the papers what was to be his last attempt to vindicate himself. Addressed specifically to the *Saturday Review*, but in reality to all those people of all professions who had slandered and mocked him, it was a bitter and withering testament.

"If the *Saturday Review* wishes to know what I do resent, let it be understood that I resent all manner of impertinence, brutal horse-laughs at the mention of Livingstone's name, or of his sufferings; all statements that Livingstone is either insane or irritable . . . all statements that I am not what I claim to be—an American; all gratuitous remarks such as 'sensationalism', as directed to me by that suave gentleman, Mr. Francis Galton . . .; and all such nonsense as the Spectator has seen fit to attribute to my pen." [36]

All those people who had met Stanley and had understood him, and many other simple Englishmen who had not done so, read this letter with humiliation. They thought of the plain facts of Stanley's achievement, that Livingstone's life had been saved and his unique geographical records brought back to civilization. They thought of England's reputation for fair play and justice, and of the shabby impression that all this ingratitude must make abroad. They spoke of these things to each other, and they blushed for shame.

Among these people, one man in particular was stirred and humiliated. This man was Edwin Arnold, poet, scholar, and editor of the *Daily Telegraph*, and when it became obvious, some days after Stanley's arrival in London, that nothing was going to be done about him, he determined to try to force the Geographers' hand. On the 6th of August he wrote to Sir Arthur Helps, Clerk of the Privy Council.

"How shameful is this jealousy against Stanley and the newspapers—for having saved Livingstone and his priceless discoveries unofficially! As an old traveller—and having closely questioned the American—I do not fear to say that a cooler, finer piece of quiet derring-do was never told. But after hinting that he was a swindler—and then saying that 'Livingstone had rescued Stanley'—the Royal Geographicals have handed the great business over to a sub-section of the B.A. at Brighton; Stanley does not care—but think how mean and petty it all appears to the Americans! Can you not whisper in the right ears that the hour is passing when this pitiful behaviour might be neutralised? A gracious note from Court—a kindly compliment from the good Queen's lips— would sweep the gathering evil of this stupid officialism away, and be re-echoed in proud pleasure from American hearts. I write this to you as at once sympathetic and in- fluential, and write it 'out of my own head'—but indeed some such thing ought to be done." [37]

The precise record of what Sir Arthur Helps did on receipt of this letter has not survived, but the result of his actions appeared soon afterwards. On the 27th of August, the day on which Stanley published his long vindication in the papers, he re- ceived a note from the Foreign Secretary, Lord Granville, send- ing him on the Queen's behalf a magnificent gold snuff-box, inlaid with blue enamel, and bearing the royal cypher, "VR", in diamonds, emeralds, and rubies. The queen herself, said Lord Granville, wished him to know that she admired and thanked him for his services to England.

Ten days after this he was invited to Dunrobin, the home of the Duke of Sutherland in Scotland, and presented to the Queen herself. He travelled north with Sir Henry Rawlinson, who kept him in his place by telling him how to behave in the royal presence, and warning him that nothing the queen said to him was to be published. But the presentation was a triumphant moment in Stanley's life, and if he had suffered in the days be- fore, the event itself more than made up for it.

The Queen spoke to him for about ten minutes in a small drawing-room at twelve o'clock in the morning. He was introduced by Sir Henry Rawlinson, and knelt and kissed hands, and then rose and answered questions about his journey and Dr. Livingstone. The thing that surprised him most about the Queen was her size, for he had never imagined that she would be smaller than he was. It put him at his ease, and as he talked he stared into her eyes, deeply moved by her natural dignity and regal manner.

After this, honours tumbled upon him from every quarter of the kingdom. The Fishmongers Company gave a dinner for him, and the Turners Company made him an honorary Freeman. The Lord Mayor of London gave a banquet in his honour at the Guildhall, and many other cities, including Glasgow, Edinburgh, Manchester, and Liverpool, also entertained him. The town of Hamilton—Livingstone's birthplace—awarded him the Freedom of the Borough, as did the city of Inverness. He did not know what this Freedom meant, but all the same he was glad to receive it. Wherever he went he gave lectures, drawing huge crowds, speaking earnestly of Dr. Livingstone and hitting out at Dr. Kirk. Even the officers he had known in Abyssinia, some cornets of the Scinde Horse, and a few formerly abusive majors, clubbed together and gave him a banquet. This was the sweetest fruit of all.

Finally the Royal Geographical Society capitulated, and at a banquet in Willis's rooms in St. James's Square gave him their highest honour, the Victoria Medal. According to the rules of the Society, this should not have been awarded until the spring, but Stanley was given it at once—an honour never before paid to any other explorer. Not only the Society as a whole, but Sir Henry Rawlinson personally had come to regret the events of the last few weeks, and Sir Henry gave a complete, humble, and sincere apology for having caused him so much distress. Sir Henry may have realized when he saw Stanley at close quarters at Dunrobin that his odd behaviour and rough ways were due only to simple background and self-education and, seeing this, perhaps he had felt ashamed.

In a speech of thanks to the Society, Stanley spoke with the same abrupt *naïveté* that he used always. He had to admit, he said, that he had dreamed of being given a gold medal by the Society, and he was very pleased the dream had now come true. It was all Dr. Livingstone's fault, for the Doctor had told him the Society would honour him in this way, and if they had failed to do so they would have caused the Doctor great dis-

appointment. Much had been said about his aspersions on Dr.
Kirk. He understood that Dr. Kirk had now received a very
friendly letter from Dr. Livingstone. He was delighted to hear
it. As long as Dr. Livingstone thought he was injured by Dr.
Kirk, then he, Stanley, would think so too. But if Dr. Livingstone now felt that Dr. Kirk was his friend, then Dr. Kirk was
a friend of his also.

At the end of the banquet there was much handshaking and
back-patting, and both Stanley and Sir Henry Rawlinson must
have slept more serenely that evening than they had done for
a long time. For Stanley it was virtually the end; he was soon
to embark for America, where he was certain of being understood and appreciated, and after a lecture tour he was to go back
to work on other assignments. For Sir Henry Rawlinson it was
virtually the end too, and with regard to the events of the past
twelve months he had only one more detail to attend to. This
was a domestic matter for the Geographical Society, and had
nothing to do with Stanley, but concerned his own Relief Expedition. He had to make up the accounts for it and issue them
to subscribers, and he had also to make final settlements with
its four officers—Dawson, Henn, Oswell Livingstone, and New.

Over the Relief Expedition there had been the most frightful
commotion ever recorded in the history of the Society. At the
beginning of May, when the first news of Stanley's success was
received in London, Sir Henry Rawlinson had not supposed it
would make any difference to his expedition. If Livingstone [38]
had reached Tabora and rescued Stanley, well and good. The
Relief Expedition could then visit the Doctor all the more easily,
and having supplied him with everything he needed, they
might be able to give a few odds and ends to Stanley. But
Lieutenant Dawson would not care whether Livingstone had
met Stanley or not. The Expedition's instructions were clear,
and there was no reason for Dawson not to obey them. He was
to find Livingstone and relieve him. If necessary, he was to
bring him home.

When the true details of the situation began to be known in England, and it became obvious that Dawson might easily meet Stanley at Zanzibar, people began to wonder what would happen. A Mr. Danby Seymour asked Sir Henry Rawlinson at a meeting what orders had been given Dawson for such an emergency. Sir Henry replied that the answer was none, for he had not thought that this contingency was imminent.[39] As to what Dawson should do now, he relied on him to make whatever decision was appropriate, but presumably he would stick to his instructions and go on to Tabora. Any journey by Stanley was really no concern of theirs.

On the 13th of June, however, Sir Henry Rawlinson received a personal telegram from the Governor of Bombay telling him that Stanley was near the coast with Livingstone's papers, and that Dawson had retired because there was no difficulty in sending goods up to Tabora. At the same time he received a letter from Henn's father asking him what the situation was, and he wrote back on the 17th, saying that the Expedition had been broken up.[40] He added that he supported this course, for there was no point in the party making the difficult and expensive journey up to Tabora if Livingstone was perfectly safe, and he thought Dawson was quite justified in cancelling it.

But once again Sir Henry Rawlinson found he had made a mistake and had misjudged the public's reaction to an event which concerned Dr. Livingstone. The entire British nation was outraged to hear that just because Stanley had found Livingstone, Dawson had no intention of going up to see him. The fact that the Doctor was now known to be at Tabora, perfectly accessible, a mere five hundred miles from the coast, made Dawson's conduct worse. And as a last straw it appeared that all the valuable instruments, clothes, and provisions bought by the British public were once again to be sent up in the hands of a few natives, who might steal the lot. How Sir Henry Rawlinson could agree to such behaviour was more than anybody could understand, and once more he was forced to change his ground and say something else. He regretted, he said, that Dawson had not gone up to Livingstone, and he looked forward to learning his reasons in due course.

As to the members of the Expedition itself, when they got farther away from Africa they too began to wonder if they had been right in their decisions. As they neared England they became nervous, and in spite of the excellent reasons which each one of them had found for not going up when they were at Zanzibar, they began to hope that these reasons would still seem cogent at home. The Rev. Charles New determined to publish his story first, and while he was still on board ship in the Mediterranean he penned an enormous letter to *The Times*, which he posted at Marseilles. He likened the Expedition to "an immense balloon, trembling through all its gigantic bulk, and ready to leap on its unknown course", and went on to explain how it came about that he himself had not floated up with it. When all the other members had resigned, he had offered to go forward alone. But Henn had been piqued by this, and had joined up again and forced him back into second place. This humiliation, he said, was more than his honour could stand.

Henn was furious at this, and as soon as he reached London he wrote an answer to it, but by this time the public had joined in with opinions of their own, and nobody paid much attention to him. Oswell Livingstone wrote to the papers too, championing Dr. Kirk against Stanley's accusations, and Stanley also intervened, and said that the real cause of the Expedition's failure was its fear of a couple of swollen rivers and a few drops of rain. If they had started at once and ignored the rainy season, as he had done, they might have achieved something. The only person who did not write to the papers at this time was Dawson. Having refused to travel with Stanley, and having gone round by the Cape of Good Hope, his journey had taken much longer, and it was well into the third week of August before he got home.

For many obvious reasons it had been the intention of the

Geographical Society to say as little as possible about the Relief
Expedition, and especially to say nothing officially until Dawson had returned and made them a proper report. But the
turmoil was so tremendous that they were forced to make an
interim statement on the 9th of August, and in this they gave
such facts as were known to them, inevitably criticizing Dawson by implication. When Dawson finally arrived on the 24th
and read this, he felt he had been judged in advance, and he attacked the Geographical Society in public with such venom
that they were compelled to defend themselves. In a final report
on the 16th of September they condemned him outright: not
to have gone forward himself, not to have sent up the Expedition, not even to have written a note to Dr. Livingstone telling
him what had happened were inexcusable. These were lamentable mistakes, and the Society could not condone them.

When Dawson read this he almost went off his head with
mortification. He seized a pen and wrote a wild letter to the
Daily Telegraph. The Geographical Society had wilfully tricked
him, he said. The whole Relief Expedition had been nothing
but a plot to get hold of Livingstone's papers, in which he had
been the cat's-paw. He had discovered this and foiled them, and
now he had been made the scapegoat.

But although the public blamed the Society for failing to give
proper orders, they had no sympathy for Dawson, and accepted as true the final verdict of *The Times*. There could not
be many young men, said a leading article, who could find
themselves so close to Dr. Livingstone in Africa and not go up
to him. In fact, when you thought about it, Dawson, Henn and
New must be the only three in the world.

A fascinating private correspondence exists on all this in the
archives of the Kirk family. Dawson went off to Ireland to stay
with Henn and to get some shooting, but the weather was bad
and he did not enjoy himself. Henn's was an old family house in
County Clare by the name of "Paradise", and one can imagine
the two abused and disillusioned lieutenants sitting by the fire

in the dripping evenings, drinking port and cursing the Geographical Society. Everyone had betrayed them, they wrote to Dr. Kirk. The Royal Geographical Society had stabbed them in the back, New had lied about them, Oswell Livingstone had fooled them, and Stanley, of all political bosh, had been presented to the Queen! They were going to retire and leave the Navy for ever. "Somehow or another", said Henn, "I feel a great wish sometimes to go out to Africa again. . . . I suppose you will think I am mad." Oswell Livingstone wrote to Dr. Kirk as well, and he too longed to get out of England and return to the peace of Africa.

Sir Henry Rawlinson also wrote to Dr. Kirk, giving him the other side of the picture, and so did the assistant secretary of the Society, Mr. Bates, who sent him £200 from the Society to compensate for all the extra personal expense the Relief Expedition must have put him to. The row went on and on, and it was still raging when Stanley left for America. The day before he sailed, Mr. Bates wrote again to Dr. Kirk to give him the latest news about it. The turmoil and confusion were as bad as ever, he said. The public were "wild".

Just before Stanley sailed he had one last personal triumph. This was the publication of his book, "How I Found Livingstone", a volume of more than seven hundred pages, with six maps, fifty-three illustrations by himself,[41] and his own photograph as frontispiece. It was an instant and phenomenal success, and ran into three editions before Christmas.

"It is, without exception, the very worst book on the very best subject, I ever saw in all my life," wrote Florence Nightingale to Monsieur Mohl on the 24th of November.[42] "Still I can't help devouring it to the end." And she went on to reflect that the whole episode had been rather like Humpty Dumpty, "when all our government, all our Societies, all our Subscriptions, and all the Queen's men could not set Livingstone up again!"

The best parts of the book were those describing Stanley's

fights with Mirambo and adventures with Livingstone, and the worst parts were homilies on the Relief Expedition and the behaviour of Dr. Kirk. Kirk was depicted as lazy, vindictive, and jealous of Dr. Livingstone's fame, and in spite of the fact that all these charges were disproved within six months, he hardly lived them down for the rest of his life. Even Stanley's admirers criticized him for attacking Kirk in this way, saying that such accusations ought never to have been published until they had been investigated. But, as an American journalist, Stanley was accustomed to writing exactly what he thought about people, and he refused to agree. That was how Dr. Kirk behaved, he said, and the British public had a right to know about it.

To Stanley's enemies the final outrage was his lecture tour in America, for which he was offered the gigantic fee of £10,000, exclusive of all expenses. They pointed out that this sum could bring him an income of £300 a year for life, while Dr. Livingstone, after thirty-five years in Africa, still had no salary from the Government or even the promise of a pension. This inequity between the two men was the worst injustice of all, and proved all that people had said about Stanley—that he had begun life as a *flâneur*, turned into a coxcomb, flowered into a mountebank, and was now going to make his fortune out of Dr. Livingstone, marry, and settle down.

Stanley did not answer these slanders, having learnt to ignore them, but the trouble was, too, that he had become so reserved and abrupt that he never gave his critics an opportunity to change their minds. If he had met them as friendly equals and given them a chance to see what he was really like, they might have realized that much of his trouble was nothing but extreme shyness and ignorance of the English way of life, and that all he wanted was a little sympathy and understanding. But Stanley refused to have anything to do with people after they had criticized him, and with the best will in the world it was impossible to persuade him to do so. Dr. Horace Waller, brother-in-law of Dr. Kirk and an old friend of Livingstone's, who talked to

New York Herald

JAMES GORDON BENNETT

Stanley for five hours soon after he arrived and saw him many times afterwards, found him absolutely impossible. All members of the Relief Expedition came to the final conclusion that he was an unmitigated scoundrel, and many other people who were disinterested in the Society's squabbles found him boorish and rude. Even the great friends of Dr. Livingstone, Mr. and Mrs. Webb of Newstead Abbey, to whom Stanley told all the secrets of his illegitimacy and upbringing, found him so difficult with strangers that they always entertained him alone. He was a perfect porcupine, Mrs. Webb declared, and one day when some neighbours dropped in and he was fierce with them and frightened them away, she lost her temper and called him a porcupine to his face.

Stanley accepted this in a friendly spirit, knowing that he deserved it, but he could not change his ways.

For the truth was that he no longer cared what English people said about him, and was content to let them think what they liked. If the Queen had received him and given him a gold snuff-box, then there could not be much wrong with him, and his enemies could say what they chose. He was particularly pleased with the snuff-box, and as he used to do with the portrait of his foster-father many years before, he spent long periods turning it over in his hand and looking at it. One day he counted the diamonds in the top of it, and found that there were more than five dozen of them. It was indeed a present from a Queen!

But the Queen herself had not been very impressed by Stanley. The day she received him she wrote to the Princess Royal in Berlin telling her about it.

"I have this evng. seen Mr. Stanley, who discovered Livingstone, a determined, ugly little Man—with a strong American twang." [43]

Stanley would have been hurt to know that she had thought him ugly. But her description of his accent might have pleased him, for it proved the success of his disguise as a foreigner, and was a true hall-mark of his adopted country.

And he was soon to arrive in the United States. His last civic reception was at Liverpool, a farewell banquet by the Mayor and Corporation on November the 9th, and the same evening he set sail for New York with Kalulu. He shook the dust of Britain off his feet, and resolved that never again would he allow upper-class Englishmen like Sir Henry Rawlinson to get the better of him.

As for his reception in America, this was assured, and Steinway Hall was already booked for his first lecture in New York. Best of all, at long last he would once more shake the hand of his chief, that prince of moguls, James Gordon Bennett, to whom his accent would be normal and his odd, round visage the face of a friend. James Gordon Bennett had earned him all this celebrity and wealth, and he would not forget it. It was fourteen years, eleven months and eleven days since Stanley had shipped from the same port for America as a cabin-boy on the "Windermere". At this moment he was just completing his thirty-second year, but he had never known when his birthday was [44] or even the year of his birth. He was inclined to think he was two years younger than he actually was, and once told someone that his birthday was in June, although actually it was on the 28th of January.

Chapter Seventeen

IN the summer of 1872, as Stanley had sailed from Zanzibar for the Seychelles, Bennett's father, founder and owner of the *New York Herald*, died in New York, at the age of seventy-seven. This was an important event, because he was one of the richest and most influential men in the United States. Many people were especially interested in it, for although Bennett Jr. had managed the paper since 1866, he was said to hate journalism and to wish to give it up. If he sold the *Herald*, every major newspaper in New York would bid for it, and there would result the biggest journalistic battle for years.

But James Gordon Bennett Jr. had not the slightest intention of selling the *Herald*, and his one ambition was to run it himself and make it even more fabulously successful than it was already. His six years of management had given him a liking for journalism, and shown him also that he had a flair for it. The *Herald* had made him rich, too—reputedly the third richest man in America—and he relished the power that money and the ownership of a newspaper could give him. To sell the *Herald* would be the last act of his life. His income alone was a million dollars per year.

Bennett was born in 1841, just five months after Stanley, the eldest son of a Scots father and an Irish mother, both of whom were poor emigrants to America. His mother hated the United States, and when her husband became a millionaire she left America and lived in France. For this reason, Bennett had no settled home, and he spent a rootless youth, travelling endlessly between Paris and New York, educated by cringing tutors and surrounded by fantastic wealth.

He grew tall and boney, with a long face, dark hair, drooping moustaches, and black, suspicious eyes. He was bad-mannered, common, and savage, believing only in the power of money, and despising the whole world except a few men who were richer than himself. When he was bored he drank, and if he became excited at these times, he did wild and terrifying things. Sometimes he fought strange men in bars, simply because they looked at him, and at other times he drove a carriage and four like a madman through the streets of Paris in the dead of night, flinging off his clothes as he went until he reached home completely naked. If people complained, he silenced them with a stream of dollars, and he was so rich that in the end he always got his way.

When he took over management of the paper at the age of twenty-five, he behaved like a tyrant, demanding obedience to his slightest whim, showing violent jealousy to any member of the staff who became too successful, and surrounding himself with spies and toadies. He refused to read anything that was badly written, but he forbade the use of typewriters, writing his own letters illegibly on special paper of robin's-egg blue. He detested people of gentle upbringing and intellectuals with artistic mannerisms, and he once dismissed a music critic for persistently refusing to have his hair cut. He played cruel tricks on people to test their loyalty, and if they complained he dismissed them at once. On one occasion he sacked all the senior members of the staff because someone told him they were indispensable.

But despite all these demonstrations of monomania, he soon proved that he was no feeble seed of a napoleonic father, but a second Napoleon himself. He ran the *Herald* like a machine, and made the staff work like demons. He developed a whole new range of methods which became standard journalistic technique. He devised the idea of the "interview", was the first owner of a daily newspaper to publish illustrations, and long before his competitors, he realized that the most expensive telegram over the Atlantic cable would repay itself if it brought important news to the *Herald* first. He also built a fleet of fast yachts which cruised about the coast of New York on the lookout for steamers from abroad. When they sighted one they intercepted it, learnt the latest news, and raced back with a report to the *Herald* office. Bennett often published foreign information so far ahead of any other newspaper that for several editions no one believed it was true. His methods became known as the "New Journalism", and the *Herald* became the direct forerunner of the picture newspapers of to-day. Spicy news, up-to-the-minute reports, amusing gossip, and huge sales were the characteristics of this technique, and for thirty years Bennett inspired it and led the field.

But in addition to this exceptional capacity for business, Bennett had one touch of real genius. In the realm of world events he was able to divine what and where something was going to happen long before any other person suspected it. Of all the secrets of journalism, this is the greatest, and Bennett possessed it to an uncanny degree. Over and over again on a whim or a hunch he would send a correspondent to some remote corner of the globe, and the very day the man arrived there, something extraordinary would happen. "If the Grand Llama of Tibet 'shuffles off this mortal coil', a reporter of the *Herald* is present in the death chamber to feel the pulse of the dying sovereign," [45] wrote the editor of the *Tennessee Nashville Union* about this flair on one occasion. Although this story was a joke, the comment behind it was true.

The finding of Dr. Livingstone was Bennett's supreme demonstration of this genius, not so much for the scheme itself, as for what occurred when he touched it. The original idea may not have been his own, but that of the *Herald* agent in London, Colonel Anderson. But the moment Bennett heard about it, he saw it was a masterpiece, and by magical instinct he did the one thing which caused it to succeed.

Any ordinary man would have sent Stanley off at once. For no obvious reason, Bennett delayed him and sent him all round Asia Minor first. Stanley could never understand why Bennett had done this, and in all probability Bennett never knew the reason for it himself. He just felt in his bones that the result would be to his advantage, and this proved to be the case.

If Stanley had gone straight to Ujiji within a few months of leaving Paris, he would never have found Livingstone, for the old explorer would have been three hundred miles away in dense jungle on the other side of Lake Tanganyika. Because of the delay, a year later he reached Ujiji only thirteen days after Livingstone had arrived.

A similar advantage was gained in England from the postponement. If Stanley had brought word of Livingstone in 1870, he would have caused a nine days wonder, but little more, for at that time nobody was worrying about the Doctor. But eighteen months later the whole world was anxious about him, and Bennett was able to produce news of his safety at the precise moment when the greatest number of people wanted to buy it.

Stanley believed that the strange delay which saved Livingstone's life was a true manifestation of Providence, but Bennett told him this was bunkum. So far as Bennett was concerned, the whole affair merely demonstrated once again that with enough money you could do anything. It also proved he was a genius, and this, in fact, was exactly what he was.

For the first nine months of 1872, as one by one Stanley's letters arrived from Africa, Bennett enjoyed himself increasingly. As everybody laughed at the *Herald* Expedition, he made fun of it too, and he filled as many columns of the *Herald* with other people's jokes as he did with Stanley's despatches:

"A war is raging fiercely between kings OKO-JUMBO supposed to be a relation of MUMBO-JUMBO, and JA-JA [he reprinted from the *Boston Traveller*]. The hills and vales echo with the sound of clashing arms, and the smoke of roasting captives sickens the noonday sky. All Africa stands aghast . . . and long before this 'Stanley' has probably made his appearance on the field as a war correspondent." [46]

Bennett published little messages to Stanley and wished him a happy New Year; he also twitted the Royal Geographical Society and Sir Henry Rawlinson about their Relief Expedition. Expeditions went to his head, and he announced that he had sent another one up the Nile and a third to the backwoods of America. The first of these probably existed and was to interview Sir Samuel Baker who was exploring the Sudan; the other was nothing but an invention. It was said to be commanded by a special correspondent in a canoe, who was not to return until he had found the sources of the Mississippi.

As Stanley reached the shores of Europe and the whole world talked about the *Herald* Expedition, Bennett enjoyed himself extravagantly. Lewis Noe, the manservant whom Stanley had taken to Turkey in 1866, wrote maliciously about Stanley to Bennett's rival, the *New York Sun*. He knew for a fact, he said, that Stanley was a swindler and had forged the two letters to Bennett which supposedly came from Dr. Livingstone. Bennett had published these in facsimile, and Noe claimed that the writing in them was Stanley's to a stroke. To prove this he sent two letters of Stanley's which he had received himself a few years earlier.

The *Sun* in its turn reproduced these in facsimile, and as a retort, Bennett facsimilied every single letter of Dr. Livingstone's in the United States. He covered two entire pages of the *Herald* with them, and showed that the writing in all of them was identical, and exactly the same as that of the two written to himself.

When Bennett heard of the statement in the *Carnarvon Herald* that Stanley was a Welshman, he replied banteringly that Stanley was no Taffy Leek or ap Jones, but a native of Missouri. When there was no special controversy going on, he wrote leaders in praise of himself. And he commiserated with the other New York newspapers for not rescuing Dr. Livingstone, but told them not to mind too much. It was true that he made a few extra million dollars from increased circulation, but as equal members of the journalistic fraternity, the honour and glory was shared by them all.

As time went on, however, and the first general astonishment passed, James Gordon Bennett got bored. And when Stanley began to be acknowledged in England, and finally was received by the Queen and presented with a snuff-box, Bennett's boredom turned to annoyance. It was one of the strictest rules in the office that no correspondent was ever mentioned by name. In this case it was inevitable for Stanley's to be revealed, and Bennett was prepared to put up with it so long as the *Herald* got the benefit. But there was no need to carry things too far, and Bennett began to think they had gone this distance when Stanley was congratulated by Queen Victoria. Bennett had no respect at all for the British monarchy, but he knew the value of its prestige and he thought that if anyone was presented, it should have been himself. Who the hell was Stanley, after all? He was nothing but a little runt nobody had ever heard of. It was Bennett who had conceived the *Herald* Expedition, Bennett who had paid for it, and Bennett who had earned these congratulations. Stanley had done nothing at all except walk a few miles into the jungle and then come back again.

The more Bennett thought about this, the more annoyed he felt, and when he learnt on the 1st of October that Stanley was to receive fifty thousand dollars for a lecture tour, he became enraged. This sum was equivalent to the entire cost of the expedition. He, Bennett, ought to have this money. But Stanley was going to get it. In the first place, Stanley had been given a free trip to the tropics plus a boat ride on Lake Tanganyika with Dr. Livingstone, and now he was going to scoop the profit by drivelling about it to a few upper-crust matrons at Steinway Hall.

Bennett went around like a tiger, and as the time of Stanley's visit approached he became dangerous. But the excitement in New York about Stanley was so exceptional that Bennett decided to bide his time and pounce on him later.

So when Stanley arrived he was shown into Bennett's office at once, and was waved into a chair and given a cigar.

Stanley reached New York on the afternoon of the 20th of November on the steamship "Cuba", and at long last received the welcome of his dreams. At the Narrows he was met by one of the *Herald* steam yachts, decked with bunting and flying a colossal banner on which was written "WELCOME HOME, HENRY M. STANLEY!" in letters five feet high. As he neared the yacht, he saw it was packed with friends, including his old chief from the London office, Colonel Finlay Anderson, and they all shouted and waved to him, and called out, "Mr. Stanley, I presume?" and told him to come on board and join them. When he did so he was received ceremoniously by a delegation from the Geographical Society of America, the leader of which stepped forward and read an address of welcome from a roll of parchment. As he reached the Battery and once more trod on American soil he was boisterously acclaimed by a huge crowd, and the Mayor himself in a silk hat came down the quay and welcomed him solemnly.

At the Battery all quarantine formalities were waved aside and he was swept off in a special carriage to the *Herald* office, where he was whisked up to Bennett like a prince. He was then taken off by his friends and drawn in procession at the head of a long string of carriages to the Fifth Avenue Hotel. When he went up to his suite he found so many reporters there that he could hardly see the walls, and there were such quantities of flowers that the room was like a tropical forest.

He sent for his trunks, and as soon as they arrived he unpacked them and showed everybody his trophies. There was the famous snuff-box from the Queen; a gold medal from the Turner's Company; a silver locket given him by the eldest Miss Livingstone, with a portrait of Dr. Livingstone inside it; and a gold tie-pin from the Duke of Sutherland, embellished with a cairngorm in the shape of a heart, surmounted by a pearl coronet. There was also the very cap worn by Livingstone at the time of the meeting, which the Doctor had given him as a keepsake.

Stanley then summoned Kalulu, who sang a song in Swahili and gave a savage native war dance. This uncivilized exhibition humiliated three sophisticated coloured bellhops who were crushed in a corner, but it amused the journalists very much, and they wrote almost more about Kalulu in the papers the next day than they did about Stanley.[47] At long last everybody left, and Stanley went to a restaurant and had dinner with some friends.

After dinner they went to a theatre and watched a farce called "King Carrot". Stanley himself was depicted in one scene of this, arriving in London, striding into the rooms of the Royal Geographical Society. The stage was filled with old men in stuffed shirts who tugged their beards and argued about the source of the Nile and Dr. Livingstone. When Stanley appeared they all fainted. It was not really very funny, but Stanley laughed till his jaws ached. New York was home, and it was good to be in it. He thought of Shaw, now dead under a heap of stones at Tabora, and remembered him sitting in the jungle playing "Home Sweet Home" on the accordion. At this moment he felt truly sorry for him. He thought, too, of Sir Henry Rawlinson, who was represented on the stage by a particularly old and quivering savant, and he felt sorry for him as well. Real tears ran down his cheeks. He stared at the stage, and laughed and laughed and laughed.

For the next few weeks the public enthusiasm about him was fantastic. Huge crowds came to his hotel and hung about in the lobby and outside in the hope of seeing him, while some people were bolder, and went up to his room and banged on the door incessantly until he opened it and shook hands with them. His book came out on the third day of his arrival, published by Scribner's, and every copy was sold within a week. He was photographed by Gurney's Gallery and copies were bought by the thousand, some showing him alone and some with Kalulu, sometimes in a black tie and morning coat, and sometimes in jungle clothes with a tropical background. Every paper in the United States carried articles about him, and wherever he went he was recognized and cheered.

In official quarters his popularity was as great as in public, and his rooms were like a post office with the number of invitations. Almost the first of these was one from the Lotos Club, a group of journalists and business men which still meets to-day. They offered him honorary membership and invited him to a banquet, and the event took place two nights after his arrival, on the 22nd of November. The Club at that time was in Irving Place, and the Great Parlor was lavishly decorated with flowers, the finest of which were woven into a garland containing Stanley's initials and words of welcome. More than three hundred members were present, including many other distinguished guests besides Stanley. The after-dinner speeches were brilliant, and several well-known members gave capital recitations.[48]

But whatever the vein of these effusions, when the speakers came to refer to Stanley they changed their mood, and spoke of him in a manner which repeated itself in every speech on every occasion for the rest of his visit. It was full of real praise and genuine admiration, but it contained an element of laughter as well, for there was something about him that amused people —he was so odd and small, and took himself so seriously. The Mayor of New York managed to squeeze him into Shakespeare, and quoted "Richard III": "Is Stanley safe, and still alive?" [49] This quotation was so far from the original that nobody could have recognized it, but as nobody knew "Richard III" the Mayor sat down in triumph. Mr. Whitelaw Reid, owner of the *New York Tribune*, and president of the club, made fun of Stanley, too. "We know that he is ugly, we hope that he is good," he said. Stanley was piqued by this, but everyone laughed so loudly that he found himself laughing with them.

But the greatest demonstration of Stanley's popularity was

given on the stage, and during the first weeks of December three
separate theatres gave entertainments about him. There was the
play which he had seen, called "King Carrot"; the theatrical
manager, Don Bryant, gave a series of burlesque lectures about
him in the Grand Opera House on 23rd Street; and the im-
presario Josh Hart produced a full-length saga on the *Herald*
Expedition at the Theatre Comique on Broadway. It was a
stupendous spectacle called "Africa", and on the 8th of December the entire front page of the *Herald* was taken to advertise
it. There were Arabs, natives, slaves, and cannibals. The cast
included the famous comic team of Harrigan and Hart, Stanley
was played by a well-known actor called Neil Warner, and to
add spice there were wives and concubines and a Lost Widow,
Biddy Malone, who was played by Miss Nellie Sandford.
There were nine scenes containing terrible fights between
Mirambo and the Arabs, pathetic monologues by Biddy
Malone, conversions to Christianity by Harrigan and Hart, and
a coconut shuffle by the Congo Dancers.

The drama was terrific, and in the last act it was breathtaking.
The curtain rose on grand old Dr. Livingstone at Ujiji on the
brink of death, pawning his watch to an Arab for a slice of pine-
apple. Suddenly there were explosions and wild scenes of native
excitement. The *Herald* Expedition arrived and marched endlessly backwards and forwards across the stage until it was exhausted. Stanley appeared, and, striding forward like a gladia-
tor, pushed aside a large cactus and came face to face with Dr.
Livingstone.

Then, in trembling silence, he raised his hat, held out his
hand, and spoke the four words that gave him immortality.

The Doctor was meant to reply to this, but he never succeeded in doing so, for every night there was such hilarity that
no one could hear himself speak.

Stanley went to see this saga one evening, and sat through it
to the finale without a smile, for he could not understand what
was funny about it. The laughter at the end especially mystified

him. How was he expected to behave? he wondered irritably. What should he have said? Perhaps he ought to have said nothing, but merely raised his hat and presented his visiting-card.

Stanley's first lecture was due on the 3rd of December, and long before this date every ticket was sold for the whole series. When the evening came, a huge crowd gathered outside the hall in the hope of seeing him arrive, and forty minutes before he came the entire hall was packed to capacity. Speculators who had bought tickets early moved through the crowd like eels, and many of them made enormous profits by selling their seats at the last minute at five times the original cost.

Inside the hall the stage from which Stanley was to speak was decorated with flowers and provided with a new mahogany reading-stand. At the back was a large map of Africa, and hanging from the wings were the two flags which had been flown by the expedition: the Stars and Stripes, and the red banner of the Sultan of Zanzibar. On a table to one side of the stage was a collection of native weapons and ornaments which Stanley had brought back with him, and on the other side, towards the back, were two gilt chairs. One of these was for Kalulu, the other was for Dr. Livingstone's brother, John, who lived in Canada and who had come down to see Stanley as soon as he had read of his arrival in New York. The papers had made great fun of this, and had announced that Sir Henry Rawlinson had been proved right after all, for at long last Livingstone had discovered Stanley.

Stanley was billed to give the same lecture heard by the Emperor Napoleon at Brighton, and he planned to do so exactly, except that, on the advice of his agent, he divided it into four parts, each to be given on different evenings. Because he had learnt that he was apt to get carried away and make a fool of himself when he spoke extempore, he determined to make a text of his lecture and read it, and he took great trouble to ensure that it was accurate and factual, to prevent anyone calling it a sensational story, as they had done at Brighton. When the evening came he felt calm and sure of himself, and he walked onto the stage with confidence. He bowed to the audience, laid his papers on the reading stand, took a sip of water, and began to speak.

But once more, and for the last time, he committed a terrible mistake. As though to make up for all the frivolities he had let slip before the Emperor at Brighton, he spoke more seriously than a professor, and made his whole lecture as dry as a bone. Not a single amusing story or personal comment escaped him, and he droned on with his head bent over his manuscript, rolling out facts about geography and anthropology for two interminable hours. It was as though he had indeed, been touched with a curse which made him do everything backwards. The detailed scientific discourse which he gave at Steinway Hall ought to have been given at Brighton, and the light-hearted narrative offered to the Emperor ought to have been given in New York. The lecture was a disaster, and the keenest geographer would have been bored by it.

Stanley gripped the edge of the lectern, and in a piping weak monotone, disserted on the phrenology of the Wagogo. Nobody beyond the first ten rows could hear him, and when he looked up for a sip of water after ninety minutes, all but the first ten rows had gone home.

But this was not the end of Stanley's difficulties, for in the audience there was a reporter from the *Herald* called George O. Seilhamer, who was one of Bennett's henchmen. Bennett had never told him to do anything about Stanley, but Seilhamer was astute enough to know what he was supposed to do, and the next day he wrote an article in the *Herald* which roasted Stanley to a crisp. The following evening Stanley gave a second lecture, which was even more desiccated than the first, and Seilhamer was again present, and again wrote a paralysing account of it. Bennett sent for Seilhamer the next day and reprimanded him, but in fact he was enchanted, and Seilhamer knew

it. This was just the opportunity he had been waiting for, and
if he had prayed for inspiration, he could not have thought of a
better way of getting even with Stanley than killing his lectures.

Seilhamer's articles succeeded in doing this completely.
Thousands of people read about Stanley's failure, and hundreds
who had bought tickets for the next series changed their minds
and sent them back. Stanley's third talk was a fiasco, for so few
people were present in the auditorium that he never gave it.
He went back to his hotel sick with anger and humiliation, and
tore his notes to pieces. He could not understand why Bennett
had allowed anyone to do this to him. He could hardly understand anything. The only thing he knew for certain was that
his lecture tour had collapsed, and that once again, for some
reason that was beyond him, someone had crept up behind him
and stabbed him in the back.

He could not even manage to see Bennett to find out about
it, for Bennett had left New York and gone to Paris for the
winter. Those members of the staff who had seen him off said
he had been strangely jubilant, and that as he walked up the
gangplank on to his private yacht he had looked queerly at
George O. Seilhamer and given him a leer.

Celebrities come and go in New York like comets, and after
a few weeks Stanley found himself forgotten. The burlesque
lectures about him came to an end, the curtain fell for the last
time on "King Carrot" and "Africa", and when he went into
the streets nobody paid attention to him. Another star arrived
from England—Professor John Tyndall of the Royal Institute—
and the American Geographical Society welcomed him with
busy enthusiasm. He gave a series of lectures on the nature of
light and "the error of Newton regarding the connection of
refraction and dispersion, and the possibility of achromatism".
George O. Seilhamer attended these lectures and wrote in the
Herald that they were the most charming pandects he had ever
heard.[50]

Stanley avoided Professor Tyndall,[51] and in fact avoided

everybody. On the 10th of December the Fifth Avenue Hotel was badly burnt, but there is no mention of his being there, and by that time he had probably gone into lodgings, as there is a later record of his living at 21 East 20th Street. His diary is blank at this date, and there are no further entries in it for the rest of the year.

Before his official visit as Livingstone's discoverer came to an end, he had one more engagement to fulfil. This was a banquet given by the Correspondents' Club in Washington, an important affair to which every influential person in the capital was invited, and at which there would be journalists from every branch of the literary field. Stanley quite looked forward to it, for although he had endured enough feasts to last for life, this would be the last of them; and after it he would return to the *Herald* as an ordinary correspondent. The turmoil of the last six months had exhausted him, he was still suffering from occasional bouts of fever and dysentery, and the one thing he longed for was the routine of normal work. He was sick of being famous, sick of being harried and exhibited, and above all, sick of being the butt of stupid jokes about Dr. Livingstone. All he wanted now was to be anonymous and forgotten, and for all the horseplay about Dr. Livingstone to be forgotten too.

But at this last banquet, far from hearing the last of the quips about Dr. Livingstone, Stanley was doomed to see the real beginning of them. For he was to witness the development of the joke into the universal burlesque greeting it soon became, no longer special to Dr. Livingstone or himself, but suitable for any person of any name.

The banquet took place at the Willard Hotel on the evening of the 11th of January, 1873, and among the two hundred guests who packed the tables and consumed the sumptuous dinner of ten courses with ten different wines, were two friends called William P. Copeland, of the New York *Journal of Commerce*, and L. A. Gobright, of the New York Associated Press. Mr. Copeland wrote poetry, and to distinguish the occasion he

composed an ode in trochaic dimeters after the style of "Hia-
watha" which he called "Stanlico Africanus". In it he told the
story of the *Herald* Expedition, but when he came to relate the
meeting at Ujiji, as the names of Stanley and Livingstone were
getting a bit stale by then, he inserted the name of his friend
instead. To prevent anyone thinking the poem was really by
Longfellow, he signed it Shortfellow, and as he was rather
pleased with it he had it printed at the office and bound into a
little book with a shiny brown paper cover.

The evening passed in the customary manner, and after the
coffee there were the usual toasts and speeches. Mr. Blaine, the
famous Speaker of the House of Representatives, gave an ora-
tion. Congressman Dodd gave a burning recitation of "Shamus
O'Brian", and finally William P. Copeland declaimed his ode.
There were so many cheers and interruptions that he had difficulty in saying it with feeling, but he was determined to read
all the twelve stanzas. After a struggle he eventually got to the
eleventh. Mr. Gobright sat near him, laughing as much as anybody, with no idea that his name was soon to be part of the
joke.

This climactic moment came in the twelfth stanza, when the
Herald Expedition reached Ujiji.

> "Beyond the hills where Speke and Burton
> Viewed the gorgeous Tanganyika,
> Stanley's African attendants
> Shouted 'Wallah, bana yanga!'
> See the lake of Tanganyika,
> Smell the fish of Tanganyika,
> See the City of Ujiji. . . .
> On they marched with banners streaming,
> Entered fair Ujiji—
> Met the magnates of the City,
> And the object of their searching
> Who saluted Stanley, saying,
> 'Mr. Gobright, I presume!'" [52]

When Mr. Gobright heard this he was convulsed, and
laughed so much that his chair shook, and the President might

have heard him in the White House. Although there were only eight more lines, Copeland found it impossible to finish them because of the noise, and in the end he capitulated and gave Gobright a copy of the poem instead. As it was now late, the proceedings terminated, and with a last gesture of friendly happiness, everyone joined hands and sang "Auld Lang Syne".

Stanley had not spoken during the evening except to say a few words of thanks for the honour of the banquet, and when it was over he escaped as soon as he could and went upstairs to his room in the hotel. His head was splitting and he was so tired he could hardly think. It was still less than a year since he had left Livingstone, uplifted by his companionship, and certain that he would receive the world's respect for his services to him. In those days he had longed to share this exaltation with all mankind, to pass on to everyone the nobility of Livingstone's character as he had known it, and to thrill civilization with the story of the *Herald* Expedition and the dramatic triumph of its success.

Now, after only ten months, it had come to this. A hack journalist who had probably never met one person of Livingstone's calibre in his life had even gone to the trouble of printing a cheap poem about him. All this because of Stanley's own remark, the first words that had come into his head as he had gripped Livingstone's hand at the supreme moment of his life.

Stanley opened a copy of the poem and read it through. Tears stung in his eyes, and a lump of emotion ached in his throat. Downstairs in the lobby he could hear the last of the guests departing, shouting to each other and laughing about the poem. He hated Copeland and Gobright with all the force of his being.

He took off his clothes wearily, threw them on a chair, and got into bed. The poem lay on the table beside him, and he picked it up and looked at it again. "Stanlico Africanus." African Stanley. The young lion from the old jungle. That was all they could think of to say about him. The candle flickered and his eyes swam. He could no longer see the words properly, and he threw the booklet down and put out the light.

For the joke, the burlesque, the parody, this was the beginning. But for John Rowlands, alias Henry Morton Stanley, it was the bitter, bitter end.

Three months later Stanley received orders to sail to France and report to Bennett in Paris. He left New York on the 8th of April and went to London, where he left Kalulu at school with the Rev. J. Conder at Wandsworth, and then crossed the Channel to Paris. Bennett was staying at the Hotel des Deux Mondes, and Stanley went there on the 2nd of May and received orders to go to Spain. Bennett was in a violent temper and refused to allow him any more salary than he had given him three years before when he had sent him to interview Livingstone. Stanley wrote angrily about this in his diary, but he said nothing to Bennett, for he was anxious not to seem above himself in any way, and only wished to return to normal duty.

By a strange chance, on this day when Stanley once again saw Bennett in the city in which the *Herald* Expedition had been commissioned, Dr. Livingstone died in Africa, in the depths of the jungle, although the world was not to know it for another nine months. He remained faithful in his beliefs and ambitions to the last, and still searching for the source of the Nile, expired on his knees in the act of prayer.

Ten days later Stanley arrived in Madrid, and a week afterwards went to Valencia, the very city from which he had come three and a half years earlier when he received the telegram ordering him to report to Paris. He remembered this, but seemed unmoved by its significance. He wrote simply in his diary, "Valencia, Hotel de Paris, I lived here once before in 1869." Since he was now like any other reporter and obliged to keep accounts, he made a note also of the cost of the cab from the station. He paid it with some francs left over from Paris. Including the tip, the fare came to one franc and fifty centimes.

EPILOGUE

"I met H. M. Stanley once only. I sat opposite to him, and next to his wife, at a dinner-party, circa 1900. He seemed to be living up to his reputation for strong silent manhood, and did not even say 'Mr. Beerbohm, I presume?'

"His appearance was certainly a remarkable one. I think I have never seen eyes set so straight across a face, or cheek-bones so high and so outstanding."

(Sir Max Beerbohm in a letter to the author, 1953.)

Chapter Eighteen

IN February 1874 news reached England that Dr. Livingstone was dead. His followers had removed his heart and buried it under a tree at the spot where he died near Lake Bangweolo, and had dried his body in the sun and carried it back to Bagamoyo. It had been identified at Zanzibar by a broken bone in the left arm which had been crushed many years before in the jaws of a lion.

There was a strange repetition of circumstances during the last months of Livingstone's history. Sir Henry Rawlinson made a second effort to communicate with him, but this suffered a fate almost identical to the first. In the winter of 1872, shortly after Stanley had left for America, Sir Henry sent out two more expeditions. One of these went to the west coast of Africa to march up the Congo, the other sailed to Zanzibar to follow Stanley's route to Ujiji; it was hoped that by one or other of these two Livingstone would certainly be intercepted. But although the second landed in Africa, it never really started, while the first marched as far as Tabora and then, like its predecessor, found that its task was already accomplished. Messengers reached it with the news that Livingstone was dead, and his followers arrived soon afterwards, carrying his remains to the sea.

The body was brought home and buried in Westminster Abbey on Saturday, April the 18th, and thus the life of one of the world's great missionary explorers came to a noble end. Stanley was among the pall-bearers, as was Dr. Kirk, while Sir Henry Rawlinson rode in the funeral procession. Sir Henry was no longer President of the Royal Geographical Society. The duties of this office had made life too complicated for him, and some months earlier he had resigned.

Livingstone's death caused Stanley the keenest grief he had

ever known, approached only by that arising from the separation from his foster-father fourteen years before on the quay
at New Orleans.

"I was stricken dumb [he wrote to Livingstone's daughter,
Agnes] and I cannot give you a description of the misery I
felt.

"How I envy you such a father! The richest inheritance a
father can give his children is an honoured name. What man
ever left a nobler name than Livingstone?

"Written words, my dear Miss Agnes, however eloquent
would fail to express the sympathy I feel for you, and I feel
too abashed by the subject to attempt it. The very name of
Livingstone has a charm in it for me. I loved him as a son, and
would have done for him anything worthy of the most filial.
The image of him will never be obliterated from my memory, it is so green with me when I think of the parting with
him, that I almost fancy sometimes that it is palpable, and
while I think of him I shall think of his children, more especially of his favourite daughter, and of the deep deep love he
bore for her." [53]

From this moment Stanley became a changed man. He resolved to give up simple journalism and become an explorer
and to honour his love for Livingstone by finishing his work.
He dedicated himself to the African continent, and he lived to
be acclaimed the greatest explorer of his time.

Many things became more important in Stanley's life than
the *Herald* Expedition. He kept his vow, returned to Livingstone's river, and in one of the finest journeys in the history of
exploration he traced it for three thousand miles across the continent to the Atlantic, and proved it to be the Congo. He also
founded the Congo Free State, and governed it, and in a last
herculean expedition he rescued the beleaguered Emin Pasha
from the Sudan. All these achievements earned him international fame and honour, but none of them had any meaning or

significance for him compared to the meeting with Dr. Livingstone. At the height of his fame, more than twenty years later, he spoke of Livingstone still as "... my old friend whose memory is always with me".[54]

For he had touched greatness at Ujiji in November 1871, and had lived with a man who was moved by the spirit of God.

Stanley was a strange little man, and a difficult one. He had many great attributes—complete fearlessness; inflexible determination; an exceptional memory and extraordinary capacity for work; the ability to concentrate for long periods without food or sleep; above all, the unpredictable asset of luck, of which the meeting with his foster-father on the very day of his arrival in America was a good example. But on the debit side of his character he had serious failings, too. He lacked completely all social instinct, especially in relation to women, and he was unnerved by the presence of the mildest of them. He was devoid of humour, and because of his own gigantic capacity for work and strength of will, he was inclined to be intolerant of the absence of these things in other people. He was a prude on occasions, and also a prig, and sometimes a bore. Above all, he was aggressively reserved and hypersensitive. Because of these attitudes, he was deprived of many ordinary pleasures, and prevented from achieving many simple and human things.

But if his own defects isolated him from the world, they also drove him to accomplish many feats which other people found impossible. One of these was the successful leadership of the *Herald* Expedition, for although many of his contemporaries could have taken it through to Ujiji eventually, probably none of them would have got there in time to find Livingstone alive. On this journey Stanley marched almost twice as fast as anyone else who had ever done it, and analysis of the first three recorded expeditions to Ujiji shows this conclusively.* Richard Burton, for instance—himself one of the greatest of

* See Appendix.

Africa's explorers, and the first European to visit Lake Tanganyika—travelled over the route at five miles per day. But Stanley marched at more than seven miles per day, and the speed of his return to the coast from Tabora after leaving Livingstone will probably never be equalled in any comparable journey in any epoch. When Stanley reached Ujiji in November 1871 he found Livingstone barely alive. Any other man would have failed to find him at all, for any other traveller would have reached him many weeks later, and by that time Livingstone would have been dead.

The second great benefit which Stanley's defects achieved for him on the *Herald* Expedition was the development of his warm relationship with Livingstone. If Stanley had been a fellow countryman—Dawson, perhaps, or Henn or New—and if his behaviour had been more forthcoming and normal, he would never have gained Livingstone's confidence in the way that he did. Livingstone was reserved himself, and he hated to be pressed up against other people, and although it was unfashionable to say so when he became famous, a considerable number of people thought him impossible.[55] The reason for his warmth towards Stanley was because Stanley himself was exceptionally withdrawn. As they came to know each other, a genuine friendship developed, and this was possible only because of Stanley's unusual shyness. It is certain that none of the young men of the Relief Expedition would have achieved it, and more than likely none of Stanley's contemporaries could have done so.

In all the other circumstances, however, Stanley's defects of character went against him. Although, legally, he was still a British subject, to all intents and purposes he was an American, and he felt like one and behaved like one. This was a crippling disadvantage in dealing with a man like Sir Henry Rawlinson, who was the very epitome of the bluff, condescending upper-class Englishman so disliked by many Americans. If Stanley had been brought up in England, and especially if he had come from the upper or middle classes and been given a public-school education, he would have been accustomed to men like Sir Henry and might have been able to deal with him. He ought to have been tactful and polite, and to have recognized how severely Sir Henry had been humiliated by the failure of the Relief Expedition. As it was, he could not behave like this, for it was beyond his capacity, and he did just the reverse, and put his head down and charged. He fought Sir Henry in the only manner he knew how to fight anybody: attacking him with sullen ferocity, determined to go on until he had defeated him, or until he himself had been forced to his knees.

For Sir Henry's part, too, Stanley was the worst possible type to deal with—common, nervous, and irritating, totally without *savoir-faire*, and all that ordinary Americans of that period were thought to be. He felt challenged by Stanley, long before he met him, as though Stanley's antipathetic character had impinged on his own by mystical transmission, and he made fun of Stanley while he was still unknown in Africa, many months before he returned.

But the most damaging trait in Stanley's composition was his lack of social instinct, which caused him to lose his head with people. In these circumstances, the more he tried to impress them, the less he achieved it. This was shown laughably in his book, "How I Found Livingstone", the very title of which showed his aggressive lack of self-assurance. He was a gifted journalist, with a clear and vivid style, and when he wrote without inhibition in articles for the *Herald*, he could bring the dullest subjects to life. But when he tried to be literary he became absurd, and his efforts to be Johnsonian were lamentable. Water became the "potable element"; wine, the "ruby liquid that cheers"; and shaking hands was the "interlacing of digits". When he came to express himself in public speech, the same thing happened. His *débâcles* at Brighton and New York came about for this reason—just because he was trying too hard to be something he was not. The famous four words of the greeting were caused by this same failing too.

These four words, which came to symbolize to the world the great encounter at Ujiji, haunted Stanley like a bad dream, and he began to think that they alone had been the whole cause of his difficulties. This was not the case, for the root cause of the mean treatment meted out to him in England was the unexpected competition of the Relief Expedition, and the uncontrolled jealousy of Sir Henry Rawlinson. So far as the Royal Geographical Society was concerned, even if Stanley had said nothing, they would have felt the same about him.

But as the years went by, and the jokes continued inexorably, he became convinced that if he could have said anything else, the whole outcome of the expedition would have been different. People would have taken him seriously, and no one would have dared to laugh at him or doubt his story.

There was some truth in this theory. For although some people thought the words of the greeting were pleasing and apt, there were others who regarded them as ridiculous, and to these people at the time they proved that the whole story was a fantastic invention.

For many years nobody dared speak to him about it, for he was too famous and too reserved for anyone to take liberties. But towards the very end of his life a generation grew up to whom his remark was nothing but a cliché, and people began to wonder if he had really said it. At last somebody actually asked him if he had done so.

He had bought an estate near Pirbright, and the person who put the question to him was the rector of the nearby parish of Worplesden. The rector was Duncan Crookes Tovey, a former master at Eton College, and Stanley sometimes worshipped at his church.

"You didn't really say 'Dr. Livingstone, I presume?' did you, Sir Henry?" asked the rector.

Famous though Stanley now was, honoured by the Queen

with a knighthood, the friend of princes, and a living hero to almost every schoolboy in the world, he felt strangely humiliated by this simple question.

He stared at the rector with his odd, grey, wide-set eyes, and for a while did not answer. Finally he admitted it.

"Yes," he said abruptly. "I couldn't think what else to say." [56]

Appendix

COMPARATIVE TABLE OF EXPEDITIONS TO UJIJI WITHIN THE YEARS 1858–73

Ref.	Party.	Force.	Cost.	Arrived Ujiji.	Time from coast.	Age at that date.
L.R.C.A. I. 4, note, and 129. Speke 151 and 193.	Burton and Speke	132 men 33 asses	£3,200	13 Feb. 1858	7½ months	37 31
H.I.F.L. 72 and J. Francis 282	Stanley	192 men 27 asses 2 horses 1 dog	£9,000	3 Nov. 1871	8½ months	30
A.A. 36, 70, 72, 237	Cameron	240 men 22 asses	£11,101	18 Feb. 1873	11 months	29
L.L.J. 191, H.I.F.L. 655	Relief Expedition	250 men (potentially)	£5,857	—	—	—

	Total distance.	Actual time travelling.
Burton and Speke . .	955 miles	6 months, 10 days
Stanley	975 miles	4 months, 15 days
Cameron *	825 miles	6 months, 18 days

* Cameron was in charge of Sir H. Rawlinson's second relief expedition. He met Livingstone's body at Tabora and sent it back to Bagamoyo. He himself went on to Ujiji to retrieve some of Livingstone's papers which had been left there.

Notes and References

PART I

Page

3   1   This date is from Stanley's diary. In "How I Found Living-stone" he gives it as the 16th.

    2   According to the records of the Grand Hotel, Bennett's rooms were the present numbers 34–36, directly over the famous Café Restaurant de la Paix. At that time the Place de l'Opéra was called the Place du Nouvel Opéra.

5   3   "Heyday in a Vanished World". Bonsal, p. 174.

    4   "The James Gordon Bennetts". Don C. Seitz, p. 303.

    5   "The House of Harper". Pub. 1912, p. 352.

    6   "The James Gordon Bennetts," Don C. Seitz, p. 204.

6   7   "How I Found Livingstone". By H. M. Stanley, Preface.

    8   Records of the Paris Meteorological Office.

    9   See *Scribner's Monthly*, Vol. 5, p. 105, Nov. 1872.

    10   Bowles Bros. were American bankers. They had a reading-room attached to their bank, which was in the Rue de la Paix.

7   11   Bradshaw's Guide, 1869.

8   12   Certificates of birth were not kept in Wales in 1841, and this date is taken from the certificate of baptism. A certain Dr. Evan Pierce of Denbigh is said to have been present at the birth and during Dr. Pierce's life-time it was often stated by writers on the subject that the Doctor would confirm the date of the 28th of January, 1841, and would show anyone interested the entry of Stanley's birth in his case-book. But the present writer has found no record of anyone ever having seen this. Dr. Pierce did exist, however, and lived in Salisbury Place, Denbigh, and practised there but he had no children, and it is not known what happened to his papers when he died.

    13   Illegitimacy was extremely common in Wales at this time, and in 1842 the average rate in North Wales was 12.3 per cent above the overall average for England and Wales. See reports of the Commissioners of Inquiry into the State of Education in Wales, 1847 (Ministry of Education Library).

    14   This account of Stanley's father's death is according to Emil Ludwig in *T.P.'s Weekly*, London, 17th of December, 1927 (in the Wellcome Historical Medical Library) and also to the Denbigh local doctor at the time (who was present at Stanley's birth), Dr. Evan Pierce. See a letter to the Editor of the

Page

Denbigh Free Press, 9th February, 1889, from Dr. Pierce. There is no record of the death of any John Rowland in the parish registers for the year 1841, however, and the first such record is entry no. 323, 28th January, 1843. This substantiates to some extent Stanley's statement in his autobiography that his father died in 1843, but the author does not believe that this John Rowland was Stanley's father, because the Christian name of *his* father (i.e. the former's grandfather) is given in the register as William, and there has never been any doubt that Stanley's grandfather was called John. Stanley would have said that his father died in 1843, because he knew that his father's death had taken place a few months after his own birth and he himself always believed that he was born in 1843.

8 [15] He was buried at Denbigh on 22nd June, 1846, aged 75. See parish register of burials, entry no. 567.

[16] This school was in the crypt of the local church, St. Hilary's, and was administered by a Trust and known as the "Denbigh Free Grammar School". It was established in 1726/27, and was discontinued in 1846. See Part III of Reports on Education in Wales, 1847, at the Ministry of Education Library.

9 [17] Records of St. Asaph workhouse, County Archives, Flints.

[18] The whole of this report is in the Ministry of Education Library, London.

10 [19] "Mavor's Exploded Spelling Book" (as the inspector called it) was already in its sixteenth edition in 1805. Its full title was "Mavor (William) The English Spelling Book, accompanied by a progressive series of easy and familiar lessons intended as an introduction to the first element of the English language."

11 [20] From the same report—see 9 [18] above.

[21] In his autobiography.

[22] With the exception of Stanley's first year, the inspector was a barrister called Jelinger Symons, a man whom Stanley remembered as being friendly and wise (Autobiography, p. 532).

12 [23] "H. M. Stanley, his Early Life". Cadwallader Rowlands, 1872, p. 52.

13 [24] Workhouse records, County Archives, Flints. This child was described as "Emma Jones, Alias Parry, a deserted bastard, born in 1843". She entered the workhouse on 14th June, 1851, and left in 1857 to become a domestic servant in St. Asaph.

[25] Stanley's autobiography, p. 29.

[26] Mrs. Jones is buried in Bodelwyddan churchyard, North Wales. The information about the brass plate is from the *Free*

Page

Press (Denbigh), April 1886, repeated in the same paper, 23rd January, 1954.

13 [27] Stanley's autobiography.

14 [28] County Archives, Flints.

[29] He did go to an uncle called Moses Owen, the son of Aunt Mary, who was a schoolmaster at a National School, but the school was at Brynford and not Holywell, and he did not go there immediately after leaving St. Asaph, but about two months later.

15 [30] Stanley's autobiography, p. 44.

16 [31] This letter is in the Wellcome Historical Medical Library, Euston Road, London.

19 [32] Stanley's autobiography, p. 83.

[33] Ibid., p. 84.

[34] Ibid., p. 78.

23 [35] Ibid., p. 89.

25 [36] See an interesting letter in this connection to Elliot Stock from Stanley on the subject of the spurious biography by Thomas George, 9th December, 1893. The Wellcome Historical Medical Library.

31 [37] Records of the Navy Department, National Archives, Washington, D.C.

33 [38] See the *North Wales Chronicle*, 22nd December, 1866. By an odd chance, six weeks earlier, on 2nd November, the same paper carried a copy of a letter, written by Stanley to the *Levant Herald*, in protest against his treatment by the bandits, under the title of "Outrage to American Travellers in Turkey". No one connected Stanley (who was appearing as John Rowlands) with this event, however.

35 [39] "Sixty Years in the Wilderness". Lucy, Series 2.

36 [40] B.M. Dept. of MSS. Cat. Add. 37463, ff. 407.

[41] There is a copy of this letter in the Livingstone Memorial at Blantyre. Part of it is reproduced in facsimile in "H. M. Stanley, his Early Life" by Cadwallader Rowlands (1872), p. 92. The original was destroyed accidentally by its owner about 1932.

[42] Stanley's autobiography, p. 244.

40 [43] Stanley's height is given in his enlistment records of the U.S. Navy, 19th July, 1864 (National archives, Washington, D.C.). Lucy, in his "Sixty Years in the Wilderness", gives a good description of how Stanley appeared to a stranger. A pair of Stanley's boots is in the Relics Department of the Royal

Page

Geographical Society, and the size is equivalent to English size 8.

41 [44] "H. M. Stanley, his Early Life". Cadwallader Rowlands, p. 91.

[45] *Scribner's Monthly*, Vol. 5, p. 105, Nov. 1872.

[46] Stanley's autobiography, p. 249.

52 [47] These drafts were for such enormous sums that in spite of his instruction to spend any amount that might be necessary, Bennett protested against them and sent them back to Zanzibar. Webb and the merchants were furious, and started legal action against Stanley, but he was by that time safely in the interior. When Bennett received Stanley's first letter from the jungle, however, he changed his mind, and by the time Stanley got back to Zanzibar the drafts had been honoured and everything was all right.

54 [48] See pp. 27–28 of the first edition of "How I Found Livingstone". Also, Rawlinson to the Royal Geographical Society, 13th November, 1871.

[49] Kirk to Livingstone, 20th October, 1870. A hitherto unknown letter in the possession of Miss Livingstone Bruce.

55 [50] Bombay was given a fine uniform commensurate with his rank, but he lost it thirty-five days after they started. "He was utterly demented in consequence" (Stanley's diary, 24th April).

[51] For 5th February, 1871, the daily record of the Mission at Bagamoyo contains the following entry: "Mr. Stanley voyageur americain et rédacteur du 'New Herald' a debarqué à Bagamoyo, il fait visite à la Mission et prend le repas du soir à la Mission. Le Père Horner fit servir, en son honneur, une bouteille de vin de champagne, laissée à la Mission par Mr. de Vienne, Consul de France à Zanzibar."

56 [52] In Stanley's record of his accounts these figures are given in dollars. The dollar in Zanzibar was the Maria Theresa dollar, worth, according to Dr. Kirk, 4.75 to the £, but its value was never fixed by any standard, and for practical purposes it may be considered to have been worth 4s., which was also the value of the U.S. dollar in 1871. The U.S. dollar of 1871 would now be worth $2.80¢ (1955).

[53] The Henry rifle was the forerunner of the Winchester and fired a .44 bullet from a 24-inch barrel. It had a long magazine which ran the whole length of the barrel and held sixteen rounds. It weighed about 10 lb. The Jocelyn (correctly Joslyn) had a .54 calibre. The overall weight was 7½ lb. and the length of barrel, 22 inches.

Page

56 **54** Burton, the first Englishman to write about the system of tribute in this area, notes that the cloth, beads, and wire, but especially the beads, were absorbed into the interior in incredible
quantities, and that this trade had been going on for many
years. The cloth came from Salem and Nashua in America and
from Manchester in England. The beads also came from
America and from Italy and Germany, each country sending
its own particular variety. The wire, which in the far interior
was considered the most valuable, came from Great Britain.
("Lake Regions of Equatorial Africa", appendix.)

57 **55** This figure represented the cost of the equipment, etc. The
entire expedition from start to finish cost about £9,000. (See
Appendix.)

56 Sillery is a champagne rarely come across nowadays and comes
from a small village of that name, south of Rheims. It is one
of the comparatively rare champagnes made only of white
grapes known as "Champagne Nature", and is of a fairly light,
dry character, appreciably lighter and drier than the normal
blended champagne.

58 **57** "How I Found Livingstone", first edition, p. 73.

59 **58** In 1845 a young French naval officer called Maizan left Bagamoyo for a journey into the interior, but he was caught by
natives on the third day out and tied to a tree and tortured to
death.

66 **59** "How I Found Livingstone", first edition, p. 309.

68 **60** This song as recorded by Stanley found its way into *Punch*,
23rd November, 1872.

70 **61** This letter, one of the only two known to have been preserved
of those written by Stanley when he was on the Livingstone
expedition, is now in the Livingstone Museum, Blantyre,
Scotland, having been given to them by the Rev. A. J. B.
Paterson who married Dr. Christie's niece. Stanley's guess at
his being back at Zanzibar in six months was not far out, since
he was back within eight months. The letter is dated 14th
August, 1871.

71 **62** "How I Found Livingstone", first edition, p. 274.

72 **63** This house or "tembe" is still standing, and it is kept in repair
by the Government of Tanganyika as a memorial to Stanley
and Livingstone, since both men lived in it together on Stanley's return journey to the coast. Livingstone, afterwards, lived
in it alone for five months, and Lieutenant Cameron also lived
in it in 1873.

Page

72 [64] This "great door" is now in the Africana Museum, Johannes-
burg, and is a fine example of the massive, studded doors
which were used in the Arab houses at that time. During the
German occupation of East Africa it came into the hands
of a private individual, who offered it to the Livingstone
Memorial in Scotland for £100, but the price was beyond
the Memorial's resources. It was then bought by the Africana
Museum.

[65] In all, Stanley had seven men who had been on the previous
expedition to Ujiji by Burton and Speke. ("How I Found
Livingstone", pp. 27 and 71, refer.)

80 [66] This map is now in the Map Department of the British
Museum.

83 [67] This cap was part of British Consular uniform, and Livingstone wore it, since he still held consular rank. To the Arabs
and natives it was the recognized badge of his status and
authority. He had several of these caps, and was very proud of
them, and often used to wear them in England. One is in the
relics department of the Royal Geographical Society, and another in the Livingstone Museum at Blantyre, Scotland.

[68] Stanley was given this cardigan by Livingstone as a memento,
and he brought it back to England with him. It is still in
possession of his family.

[69] These shoes which were French had been sent up to Livingstone by mistake, and they were all he had left. All his boots
were worn out, and he had to wait until he got back to Tabora
with Stanley before he got any more. See letter of 19th
February, 1872, from Livingstone to Waller in the Waller
Papers at Rhodes House, Oxford.

84 [70] The accepted date of this meeting is 10th November, not the
3rd, but Stanley's diary shows that the 3rd is correct. The 3rd
was the date given in his first accounts of the meeting in the
Herald, and the 10th did not appear until later. It will be remembered that he became a week out in his dates after his
attack of fever at Tabora (p. 71), and it was this that caused
the confusion. He did not discover this mistake until Livingstone pointed it out to him on what he believed was the 21st,
eleven days after the meeting, by which time he had recorded
the date of his arrival at Ujiji in his diary as the 10th. Because
of the week's error, however, the actual date was the 3rd. The
mistaken date of the 10th probably crept in to his book because, working from his diary nine months afterwards, he

Page

forgot to make allowance for the error and copied it, as it stood, into his MS.

84 [71] This figure is one given by Stanley in a lecture in 1886 ("My African Travels", British Museum).

85 [72] According to a note in Stanley's diary, Livingstone himself calculated the date of his arrival as 21st October. He did this using the Nautical Almanac which Stanley brought up to him, and he made the calculation on 14th November, a date which he was able to find out accurately from the Arabs because it was the beginning of Ramadan.

86 [73] Le Saint was a French explorer who had been at Khartoum and was on his way across Africa, heading for what is now French Equatorial Africa. He died at Abou Karka on 27th January, 1868. (Historical service of the French Ministry of Defence.)

88 [74] With regard to four-poster beds, Stanley noted the following amusing remark of Livingstone's. "He told me also that when he first obtains the privilege of sleeping on a four-poster bedstead, he cannot confine himself to one position in it but must try the luxury of rolling in it like a buffalo in his wallow, and then stretching himself diagonally, transversely, obliquely, and every other way and some times with his feet where his head ought to be, or hanging over the sides."

88 [75] Stanley's visiting-card was found among Livingstone's possessions after his death.

99 [76] Both men drank enormous quantities of tea. Stanley records that on one evening Livingstone drank thirteen cups and he himself drank eleven.

[77] "Livingstone Lost and Found", p. 542.

103 [78] Livingstone and Stanley talked about food constantly, and Livingstone used to dilate especially on the succulence of the marrow on toast which he used to have at banquets of the Royal Geographical Society, and on the Devonshire cream which Mr. and Mrs. Webb used to give him at Newstead Abbey. "You will think of me", he said to Stanley one day, "when you taste those marrow bones at the Geographical, and the Devonshire cream."

106 [79] This journal complete with its covering arrived safely in England, and is still in the hands of Livingstone's family.

107 [80] Shaw's grave is now marked by a cross a few yards from the mound of stones.

Page

111 [81] "Though I may live half a century longer, I shall never forget this parting scene in Central Africa. I shall never cease to think of the sad tones of that sorrowful word farewell; how they clouded my eyes, and made me wish unutterable things which could never be." Speech by Stanley as quoted by J. J. Ellis, 1890 (British Museum).

[82] See "Sir John Kirk", by David Williamson, p. 153.

[83] Livingstone to the Rev. W. Thompson—letter no. 68 in "Some Letters from Livingstone". Edited by Chamberlin.

112 [84] The Livingstone Bruce Collection.

113 [85] This mound of stones is still to be seen, and there is now also an inscribed tablet to Farquhar, put up in 1953 by the Government School at Mpwapwa.

PART II

120 [1] *Proc. Royal Geog. Soc.*, 16, 13th November, 1871.

121 [2] Ibid., 22nd April, 1871.

[3] *Daily Telegraph*, and others.

123 [4] *Morning Post*, and others, 28th November, 1871.

125 [5] 4th December, 1871.

126 [6] PRO. FO. 2; 49; B. Rawlinson to Enfield, 13th December, 1871.

[7] The Kirk Papers, vol. 2.

[8] In the MS. Sir Henry wrote "Unyanyembe"; it is replaced by "Tabora" here, since this name has been used throughout to denote the same place.

127 [9] PRO. FO. 2; 49; B. Granville to Rawlinson, 1st January, 1872.

[10] *The Times*, 5th January, 1872.

129 [11] *Proc. Royal Geog. Soc.*, 16, 8th January, 1872.

130 [12] *The Times*, 31st January, 1872.

131 [13] Ibid., p. 427.

[14] Ibid., p. 417.

132 [15] There had been rumours of Stanley's success a month before this, but no one had taken much notice of them. Dr. Kirk's diary shows that the first news of the meeting of Stanley and Livingstone reached Zanzibar by natives on 4th April.

134 [16] "How I Found Livingstone", p. 707.

[17] Kirk papers, Vol. 2.

135 [18] Kirk to Vivien, PRO. FO. 84; 1357.

Page

135 [19] Kirk to Vivien, PRO. FO. 84; 1357.

136 [20] "Kirk has been a sore disappointment to me. I got him the situation, and he is too lazy and indifferent to serve David Livingstone." (Livingstone to J. B. Braithwaite, 8th January, 1872; Braithwaite Collection.)

137 [21] The Livingstone Bruce Collection.

[22] There is a photo of this cottage in the Rev. New's book, "Life, Wanderings etc. in Eastern Africa", p. 519. It has now been pulled down although at least one inhabitant, alleged to be over a hundred years old, claims to remember it and to remember Stanley's visit there. It stood in the St. Louis district in Victoria, and another house called Serret House now stands on the site. (Information courtesy the Governor of the Seychelles.)

138 [23] Kirk papers.

[24] "H. M. Stanley, The Authoritative Life", by Frank Hird, p. 103. Pub. Stanley Paul, 1935.

[25] Ibid.

141 [26] See the "Memoir of Sir Henry Rawlinson", by Canon Rawlinson.

[27] *The Times*, 2nd May, 1872.

142 [28] *Proc. Royal Geog. Soc.*, 16; 241.

143 [29] *The Times*, 5th July.

[30] 2nd August.

145 [31] "Livingstone and Newstead", by A. Z. Fraser, p. 196. Pub. John Murray Ltd. 1913.

146 [32] See the footnote on p. 411 of the first edition of "How I Found Livingstone".

[33] "J. B. Braithwaite, a Friend of the Nineteenth Century", p. 196.

147 [34] PRO. FO. 84; 1366.

150 [35] *The Times*, 20th August, 1872.

154 [36] *Daily Telegraph*, 27th August.

155 [37] "Correspondence of Sir Arthur Helps", by E. A. Helps, p. 325.

157 [38] *Proc. Royal Geog. Soc.*, 16; 241.

158 [39] Ibid., 387.

[40] *The Times*, 28th August.

161 [41] The MS. of Stanley's book was destroyed during the late war, but some of his illustrations for it which he drew himself have escaped destruction. One of these (of Livingstone's house at Ujiji) is at the Livingstone Memorial, Blantyre,

Page

and several others are amongst the Waller papers at Rhodes House, Oxford.

161 [42] "Florence Nightingale", by E. T. Cook, Vol. II. Pub. by Macmillan Co., Ltd., 1913.

163 [43] Her Majesty's Library at Windsor Castle. R.A./Vic., Add. MSS. U/32.

164 [44] There is a note to this effect by Lady Stanley in one of Stanley's notebooks. See, for instance, Stanley's entry in the Marriage Records in Westminster Abbey. He was married on 12th July, 1890, and he gave his age at that date as forty-seven. Actually it was forty-nine.

167 [45] *The Nashville Union*, 27th December, 1871.

168 [46] *The Boston Traveller*, 20th May, 1872.

172 [47] See "Modern American Anecdotes", by Paul Timbs, 1873.

173 [48] "Brief History of the Lotos Club", 1895.

[49] "Richard III", Act V, Sc. 5, line 9.

177 [50] *New York Herald*, 17th and 18th December, 1872.

[51] Professor Tyndall was in fact one of the finest scientific speakers of the day, and he had an immense popular reputation in England. He received a fee of £10,000 for his lectures in America and he gave the entire sum to American charity.

179 [52] A copy of this ode is in the Wellcome Museum, Portman Square.

186 [53] The Livingstone Bruce Collection, Stanley to Mrs. Bruce (Agnes Livingstone), 18th March, 1874.

187 [54] The Livingstone Bruce Collection, Stanley to Mrs. Bruce (Agnes Livingstone), 2nd October 1896.

188 [55] "One of Livingstone's Companions, Meller (*q.v.*), who was later in Mauritius, gave testimony to a side of Livingstone's character usually kept carefully hidden; he told Anson (*q.v.*) that Livingstone was a most selfish explorer, objecting to any of his companions writing home descriptions of their doings" ("Dictionary of Mauritian Biography," No. 10, pp. 307–8, "LIVINGSTONE, David".)

The Kirk papers also contain evidence that Dr. Livingstone could be very difficult at times.

191 [56] "Donald Francis Tovey", by Mary Grierson, p. 2. Pub. Oxford University Press, 1951.

Index

"ABYDOS", 130
Abyssinia, 34, 121, 156
Adare, Lord, 38
Aden, 138
Admiralty, 130
"Africa" (steamer), 137
"Africa" (theatrical production), 174, 177
African Association, 43
Albert Lake, 44
Alphabet, Cuneiform, 122
Ambrose, Mr. Joshua, 147
American Civil War, 28-9
Anderson, Colonel Finlay, 5, 6, 167, 171
Anglo-American Press, 147
Annesley Bay, Red Sea, 35
Anson, 202
Arabs, 58, 63, 67-9, 72, 76-7, 83, 84, 85, 86, 87, 95, 103, 108, 125, 126, 136, 174, 196
Arkansas Regiment of Volunteers, 29
Arnold, Edwin, 154
Asmani, 80, 83, 107
Austria, Emperor of, 5

Bagamoyo, 54, 55, 115, 132, 185
Baker, Sir Samuel, 5, 94, 169
Bangweolo, Lake, 185
Banks, Sir Joseph, 43
Bates, Mr., 161
Batoka highlands, 45, 46
Battery, New York, 171
Bechuanaland, 45
Beerbohm, Sir Max, 184
Behistun, 122
Beke, Dr., 151
Bennett, James Gordon, Jr., 3-6, 34, 35, 94, 118, 120, 127, 129, 138, 139, 140, 144-5, 164, 165-71, 176-7, 181, 196
Bennett, James Gordon, Sr., 165
Black Sea, 5
Blackwood's Magazine, 38
Blaine, Mr., 179
Blantyre, Scotland, 198
Bombay, 6, 50, 94
Bombay, Governor of, 158
Bombay, "Sgt. Major", 55, 56, 61, 74, 77, 80, 91, 92, 100, 107, 196
Boston Traveller, 168

Bowles' Reading Room, 6, 193
Braithwaite, J. B., 146, 201
Brighton Corporation, 149
British Army, 35, 37
British Association, 143, 148, 149-53
Bryant, Don, 174
Brynford, 195
Burrowes, Dr., Mayor of Brighton, 149
Burton, Captain Richard, 6, 42, 48, 72, 122-3, 124, 187

Caernarvon Herald, 139, 169
Cairo, 94
Cameron, 192
Caspian Sea, 5
Castro, Tom, 119
Champagne, 57, 87, 197
Charles Street, London, 141
Chicago, Fire of, 119
Chobham Common, 119
Christie, Dr., 69, 87, 197
Clarendon, Lord, 119
Conder, The Rev. J., 181
Congo Free State, vii, 7, 186
Congo, River, vii, 48-9, 85, 110, 151, 152, 185, 186
Constantinople, 5, 32
Cook (Stanley's companion in Smyrna), 32
Copeland, William P., 178-9
Correspondents' Club, Washington, 178
Coutts, Baroness Burdett, 147
Coxworthy, Mr. Franklyn, 147
Crimea, 5, 37-8
Cypress Bend, 27

Daily Telegraph, 139, 143, 154, 160
Dar-es-Salaam, 59
Dawson, Lt. Llewellyn, 130, 132, 133, 137, 157-60, 188
Denbigh, 8, 30, 33, 139
Denbigh Castle, 8, 33
Derby, Lord, 119
Diary, Lett's, 95
Dickens, Charles, 119
Dilke, Sir Charles, 147
Dixie Greys, 29
Dodd, Congressman, 179
Dollar, Evaluation of, 196

Dover, 143
Dumas, Alexander, 119
Dunrobin, 155, 156

East India Company, 122
East 20th Street, No. 21, New York, 178
Edinburgh, 156
Edinburgh Journal of Science, 127
Education in Wales, 11
Emancipation Act, 43
Emin Pasha, 186
Emrik and Binger, Messrs., 147
Eton College, 190
Eugénie, Empress, 5, 149
Expeditions: Cost, 6, 52, 76, 197
    Equipment and Personnel, 51, 55-7,
        72, 80, 86, 92, 97, 105-6, 131,
        136-7
    Rate of travel, 57, 60, 64-5, 81, 84, 102,
        112-3, 115, 148, 187-8 (see also
        Appendix)
    Subsequent to Livingstone Search
        and Relief Expedition, 185

"Falcon", 50-1
Farquhar, William, 50, 56, 60-1, 63, 69,
    113, 200
Fauna, 59, 63, 78, 80, 98, 100, 114
Feragji (Stanley's cook), 73-5, 95
Ffynnon Beuno, 15
Fifth Avenue Hotel, New York, 171, 178
Fishmongers Company, 156
Fiske, Mr., 142
Foreign Office, 125-7, 130, 134, 135,
    146-7
Fort Fisher, 31
Francis, John, 9-14
Franklin, Lady, 147
Franklyn, Hales, 138
French Mission, Bagamoyo, 55, 196
Frere, Sir Bartle, 147

Galton, Mr. Francis, 149, 154
Gambetta, 119
Garrick Club, 147
Geographical Society of America, 171,
    177
Georgia, 5
German Consulate, Zanzibar, 137
Glasgow, 156
Glasgow University, 45, 131
Gobat, Bishop, 50
Gobright, L. A., 178-80
Gondokoro, 86, 94

Grand Hotel, Paris, 3, 193
Grand Opera House, New York, 174
Grant, Colonel, 94, 151
Grant, President, 79
Granville, Lord, 119, 147, 148, 155
Guildhall, 156
Gurney's Gallery, New York, 172

Hailima (Livingstone's cook), 87, 88, 95
Hamilton, Scotland, 156
Hancock, General, 33
Harrigan and Hart, 174
Hart, Josh, 174
Helps, Sir Arthur, 154-5
Henn, William, 116, 131, 132, 133, 135,
    137, 158-60, 188
Henry, G. A., 38
Henry, Prince of the Netherlands, 5
Herschel, Sir William, 128
H.M.S. "Captain", 119
H.M.S. "Penguin", 47
Horner, Father, 55
Hosmer, Dr., 138
Hotel Chatham, Paris, 139
Hotel de Paris, Valencia, 181
Hotel des Deux Mondes, Paris, 181

India Council, 122
Inverness, Scotland, 156
Irving Place, New York, 173
Italy, 128

Jerusalem, 5, 50
Jones, Elizabeth, 13, 30, 33, 194
Jones, Emma, 12, 194
Jones, Robert, 12
Jones, The Rev. John, 8
Journal of Commerce, 178

Kalahari Desert, 45
Kalulu, 71, 74, 87, 98, 137, 140, 147, 164,
    172, 175, 181
Karachi, 6
Kigoma, 59
King, Edward, 6, 7, 41
"King Carrot", 172, 174
Kirk, Dr. John (British Consul at Zanzi-
    bar), 46, 47, 53, 81, 90, 91, 104,
        105, 107, 120-2, 125, 126, 132,
        133-6, 138, 140, 156, 157, 159,
        161, 162, 185, 200, 201, 202
Kiswahili, 90
Kurum, 45

Lander, Brothers, 43
Le Figaro, 139
Le Saint, Lieutenant, 86, 199
Le Soir, 139
Liverpool, 16, 30, 33, 156, 164
Livingstone, Agnes, 106, 186
Livingstone, Charles, 46
"Livingstone Cottage", Seychelles, 137, 201
Livingstone, Dr. David, 4, 39, 44–9, 53, 60, 69, 81–110, 125, 129, 135, 141–2, 147, 151–4, 156–62, 168, 171, 174, 181, 185–88
  Appearance, 60, 69, 81, 83, 89–90, 142
  Attitude to natives, 90, 92, 101
  Consular cap, 83, 89, 198
  Early life, 44–5
  Explorations, 45–9, 85
  "Missionary Travels and Researches in South Africa", 46
  Nautical Almanac, 93, 199
  Quarters at Ujiji, 85, 87, 88, 95, 197, 199, 201
  "The Zambezi and its Tributaries", 47
Livingstone, John, 175
Livingstone Memorial, Scotland, 198
Livingstone, Mrs., 46
Livingstone, Oswell, 131, 135, 137, 138, 159, 161
Livingstone Search and Relief Expedition, 115, 125, 129–32, 133, 135, 142, 157–63, 169, 188, 190
Livingstone, the eldest Miss, 171
Llys Llanrhaeadr, 8
Loanda, 45
Locke, Richard Adams, 127
London, Lord Mayor of, 156
London Missionary Society, 45, 46
London Stereoscopic Company, 147
Lotos Club, 173
Lualaba, River, 85, 151
Lyons, Colonel, 29

Mabrouki, 72
Mackenzie, The Rev. E. F., 46
Madame Tussaud's Waxworks, 147
Madrid, 3
Magdala, 35
Mahe, Seychelles, 138
Makata, River, 63, 113
Manchester, 156
Manyuema, 4, 48, 49, 60, 89, 126
"Marmion", 118, 139
Marseilles, 138
Mary (Stanley's Aunt), 9, 15

Mauritius, 50
"Mavor's Spelling Primer", 10, 194
Medical supplies, 57
Meller, 202
Middle Street, Brighton, 149
Milnes, Monckton, 139
Mirambo, 67, 80, 81, 85, 95, 103, 108, 122, 124, 129, 141, 162, 174
Missionary Schools: Bishop Gobat's, Mount Zion, 50,
  Nassick, Bombay, 131
Missouri Democrat, 33
Moffat, Dr. Robert, 45, 46
Mohl, Monsieur, 161
Mombasa, 126, 131
Moon, Land of the, 64
Moon, Mountains of the, 58
Morris, Mr. Joy (American Minister at Constantinople), 32, 41, 50
Morris, Maria, 16–17
Morris, Tom, 16–17, 33
Mpwapwa, 59, 60, 113, 128
Murchison, Sir Roderick, 47, 120
Mweru, Lake, 48

Napier, General Sir Robert, 35
Napoleon III, Emperor, 149, 151
"New Journalism", 167
New Orleans, 19–26
New, The Rev. Charles, 131, 133, 134, 137, 159, 160, 161, 188
New York Associated Press, 178
New York Evening Post, 31
New York Herald, 34, 35, 38, 49, 57, 70, 72, 79, 88, 115, 120, 127, 128, 134, 136, 142, 144, 146, 165–71, 174, 176–81
New York Herald Islets, 93
New York, Mayor of, 171, 173
New York Sun, 127, 169
New York Tribune, 173
Niger, River, 43
Nightingale, Florence, 130, 161
Nile, River, 47, 48, 49, 85, 89, 94, 110, 136, 151, 181
Noe, Lewis, 32, 169
Norrie, Orlando, 147
Nyasa, Lake, 44, 46, 47, 48

Omar (Stanley's watchdog), 50, 57
Orton, Arthur, 119
Owen, Moses, 195
Oxford University, vii

Paris, France, 3, 5, 104, 119, 139–40
Paris Geographical Society, 139
Park, Mungo, 43
Parry, Elizabeth 9 (see also under Jones)
Parry, Moses, 9
Paterson, The Rev. A. J. B., 197
Persepolis, 6, 50
Persian Gulf, 50
Phoenix Hotel, Seychelles, 137
Pirbright, 190
Pope, The, 119
Poularde truffée à la Stanley, 140
Privy Council, 154
Prussia, Crown Prince of, 5
Pullitzer, Joseph, 33
Punch, 88, 104, 118

Quilimane, 45

Rawlinson, Major-General Sir Henry
    Creswicke, 120–31, 134, 141–61,
    164, 169, 172, 175, 185, 188–90
Reid, Mr. Whitelaw, 173
Richard III, 173
Rifles, 56, 100, 196
Rovuma, River, 47
Rowland, John, 8, 194
"Rowlands, John", 33, 139, 195
Royal Geographical Society, 43, 46, 47,
    120–9, 141–4, 148–61, 169, 172,
    190, 199
Royal Institute, 177
Royal Navy, 107, 119
Royal Pavilion, Brighton, 152
Rufiji, River, 53
Rusizi, River, 89, 92
Russell, William Howard, 37

St. Asaph, Parish workhouse of, 8–14,
    33, 139
St. Hilary's, Parish Church of, 8
St. James's Square, London, 156
Sandford, Miss Nellie, 174
Saturday Review, 88, 153
Scinde Horse, 37, 132, 156
Scott, Sir Walter, 118, 139
Scribner's, 172
Seilhamer, George O., 176–7
Selim, 50, 55, 61, 73, 77, 81, 87, 91, 97,
    137
Seychelles, 50, 137
Seymour, Mr. Danby, 158
"Shamus O'Brian", 179

Shaw, John, 55, 56, 57, 60–3, 68–71,
    75–8, 103, 107, 172, 199
Sherman, General, 33, 139
Shiloh, Battle of, 29
Shire, River, 46
Short, Right Rev. Thomas Vowler,
    D.D., 11, 21
Simbamwenni, 59–60, 114
Sioux Indians, 33
Slave trade, 43, 48, 58, 90, 109
Smyrna, 32
Snuff-box (Queen Victoria's gift to
    Stanley), 155, 163
Songs, Native, 67, 98, 107, 172
Speake, Mr., 22
Speke, John, 6, 42, 48, 80, 94
Stanley, Lord, 139
Stanley, H. M. (the explorer's foster-
    parent), 22–7
Stanley, Henry Morton:
    Birth, 8, 193
    Childhood in England, 9–18
    New Orleans, 19–26
    Cypress Bend, Arkansas, 27
    Enlistment (American Civil War), 28
    Visits mother in Denbigh, 30
    Joins American Navy, 31
    Visits Turkey, 32
    Revisits mother, 33
    Employed by *Missouri Democrat*, 33
    Employed by *New York Herald*, 35
        et seq.
    British punitive expedition, Abyssinia,
        34–5
    Attempts at courtship, 36
    Crimean War, 37–8
    Spanish Civil War, 1868, 39
    New York Herald Livingstone expedi-
        tion sets off, 55
        Reaches Simbamwenni, 59
        Reaches Mpwapwa, 63
        Reaches Tabora, 64
        Sorty against Mirambo, 67–8
        Arrives Ujiji, 82
        Greets Livingstone, 84, 198
        Leaves Ujiji with Livingstone, 97
        Regains Tabora, 104
        Bids farewell to Livingstone, 109
        Regains Simbamwenni, 114
        Disbands *Herald* expedition, 136
    Seychelles, 137
    Paris, 139
    London, 143
    Addresses British Association at Brigh-
        ton, 149
    Presented to Queen Victoria, 155
    Awarded Victoria Medal, 156

Stanley, Henry Morton (*contd.*) :
    Publishes "How I Found Livingstone",
        161
    Returns to New York, 164
    Reports to Bennett in Paris, 181
    Spain, 181
    Attends Livingstone's funeral, 185
    Returns to Africa, 186
    Appearance, 12, 24, 39, 115, 153, 163,
        173, 184, 194
    Attitude to women, 19–20, 23, 24, 36,
        40, 187
    Character, 40–1, 61–2, 163, 187–9
    Date of birth, 8, 164, 202
    "How I Found Livingstone", 161, 189
        Extracts: 57, 62, 70–1
    Journal extracts, 63, 65, 91, 101
    Lectures and speeches, 98, 139–40,
        150, 156, 175, 186, 200
    Letters, 111, 137, 153, 186
    Personal possessions on *Herald* expedi-
        tion, 57, 73–4, 76, 81, 86, 87, 89
    "Stanlico Africanus", 179–80
    Stars and Stripes (Stanley's flag), 92, 97,
        98, 115, 147, 175
S.S. "Windermere", 17–20, 164
Steinway Hall, New York, 164, 170, 176
Stone, Mr., 142
Sudan, 5, 169, 186
Suez, 39, 138
Suez Canal, 5
Susi, 82–3, 86, 91, 92–3, 109, 111
Sussex Medical Society, 153
Sutherland, Duke of, 155, 171
Swahili, 164
Sweden, 128
Symons, Jelinger, 11, 194
Syra, Island of, 36

Tabora, 56, 58, 64–76, 107–9, 124, 126,
    128, 135, 141, 200
Tabora, Sheik of, 72
Tailor and Cutter, 146
Tanganyika, Government of, 197
Tanganyika, Lake, 4, 42, 44, 47, 58, 81,
    89, 93, 126, 147, 150, 188
Teheran, 6
Tennessee Nashville Union, 167
Theatre Comique, Broadway, 174
Theodore, King of Abyssinia, 34
The Times, 37, 49, 125, 127, 140, 142,
    143, 144, 148, 159, 160
Thomas, Captain Leigh, 12, 14
Tichborne Case, 119

Tiflis, 50
Tovey, Duncan Crookes, 190
Treasury, 128, 129
Tribute, 56, 81, 92, 95, 112, 131
Turners Company, 156, 171
Twain, Mark, 33, 147
Tyndall, Professor John, 177, 202

Ujiji, 48–9, 58, 81–96, 126, 129, 141,
    142, 147, 185
Union Jack, 92, 97, 147
Unyanyembe, 72 (see also Tabora)
Usagara, 58
U.S.S. "Minnesota",

Valencia, 181
Victoria Falls, 46
Victoria, Lake, 42, 44, 94, 110
Victoria Nyanza. (See Lake Victoria)
Victoria, Queen, 155, 163
Victoria, Seychelles, 137

Wagogo, 64, 112, 128, 176,
Wakefield, Mr., 126
Waller, Dr. Horace, 162
Wapping Basin, 131
Wars: Crimean, 37–8
    Franco-Prussian, 119
    Afghan, 122
    American Civil, 27–9
    Spanish Civil, 39
Washburne, Mr. (U.S. Minister in Paris),
    139
Webb, Francis R. (American Consul at
    Zanzibar), 38, 39, 52, 70, 93, 115,
    196
Webb, Mr. and Mrs. (Newstead Abbey),
    163, 199
Westminster Abbey, 185
Willard Hotel, Washington, 178
Willis's Rooms, St. James's Square, 156
Worplesden, 190

Young, E. D., 48
Young, John Russell, 5

Zambezi, 45–6
Zanzibar, 39, 42, 47, 49, 50–2, 120, 123,
    130, 133, 185, 200
Zanzibar, Sultan of, 55, 69, 131, 175
Zion, Mount, 50